FINLEY BALL

Finley Ball

HOW TWO OUTSIDERS TURNED THE OAKLAND A's INTO A DYNASTY AND CHANGED THE GAME FOREVER

Nancy Finley

REGNERY
HISTORY

Regnery History™ is a trademark of Salem Communications Holding Corporation; Regnery® is a registered trademark of Salem Communications Holding Corporation

ISBN 978-1-62157-477-4

Library of Congress Cataloging-in-Publication Data

Names: Finley, Nancy, author.
Title: Finley ball : how two baseball outsiders turned the Oakland A's into a
   dynasty and changed the game forever / Nancy Finley.
Description: Washington, DC : Regnery History, 2016.
Identifiers: LCCN 2015040963 | ISBN 9781621574774 (hardback)
Subjects: LCSH: Oakland Athletics (Baseball team) | Finley, Charles Oscar,
   1918- | Finley, Carl A., 1924-2002. | Baseball team owners--United
   States--Biography. | BISAC: SPORTS & RECREATION / Baseball / History. |
   BIOGRAPHY & AUTOBIOGRAPHY / Sports. | HISTORY / United States / 20th
   Century. | HISTORY / United States / State & Local / West (AK, CA, CO, HI,
   ID, MT, NV, UT, WY).
Classification: LCC GV875.O24 F56 2016 | DDC 796.357/640979466--dc23
LC record available at http://lccn.loc.gov/2015040963

Published in the United States by
Regnery History
An imprint of Regnery Publishing
A Division of Salem Media Group
300 New Jersey Ave NW
Washington, DC 20001
www.RegneryHistory.com

Manufactured in the United States of America

10 9 8 7 6 5 4 3 2 1

Books are available in quantity for promotional or premium use. For information on discounts and terms, please visit our website: www.Regnery.com.

Distributed to the trade by
Perseus Distribution
250 West 57th Street
New York, NY 10107

To the memory of my father, Carl Finley, and with special thanks to our Finley Family, especially my husband Morgan D. King, my sons Doug and Morgan, and my daughter Taylor

CONTENTS

PART I:
THE KANSAS CITY ATHLETICS 1960–1968

PART II:
THE OAKLAND A'S 1968–1982

PROLOGUE

Books have been written about the Oakland A's baseball team, a team with a history of success second only to the New York Yankees. And books have been written about their charismatic owner Charlie Finley.

When Charlie Finley's niece, Nancy Finley, decided to put her memories of the Finley baseball epoch down on paper, she asked herself, "What can I say that hasn't already been said?" To her surprise, the more she thought about it, the more she realized the answer was: "Quite a lot." She could write the untold story.

A sports dynasty as spectacular as the Oakland A's of the early 1970s naturally generates a certain mythology, and at the heart of A's mythology is the caricature of an outrageous owner, the "great Satan" of MLB, a man who was "bad for baseball." But forty years after Charlie Finley's team won its third World Series title, it's time to get past the myths. In telling the Finley side of the story, Nancy brings to life one of the most fascinating characters in baseball history.

She also writes about another man, who was rarely mentioned in the sports media but was as responsible for the team's achievements as Charlie—her dad, Carl Finley, the "unseen hand" behind Charlie and the success of the franchise. Providing an insider's perspective on how these cousins—an insurance salesman and a high school principal—side-by-side took a perennial last-place team and rebuilt it into what *Sports Illustrated* proclaimed the "Team of the Century," she reveals the secrets of their success.

Starting with a "fateful midnight meeting" in Kansas City, she fills in the gaps in the story of Charlie's battles with two men who were determined to destroy him—the sports editor of the *Kansas City Star* during the A's stint in that city, Ernest Mehl, and the commissioner of Major League Baseball through most of Charlie's years with the A's, Bowie Kuhn.

And she tells the Finley side of the Mike Andrews affair, the most famous "brouhaha" in the team's history, in which Charlie was the subject of a show trial in the court of public opinion.

She also writes about a fascinating scientific explanation for Charlie Finley's fascination with colors—a rare genetic condition that might also explain his uncanny insight into the game of baseball.

Until now, much of the history of the Oakland A's from the mid-1970s to 1981 has been a blank page. But Nancy was there and knows what happened in those fateful years when free agency set the franchise back by several years.

She saw and heard things about Charlie and Carl—"those rascals"—that no one has ever told: their flirtations and affairs, their pranks, their arguments, their eccentricities, their failures and achievements.

It's a story of strong-willed men, and some women too, in the glitter and glory of an amazing baseball era—*Mad Men*, James Bond, and the Three Stooges rolled into one—a story untold till now.

AUTHOR'S PREFACE

I t felt strange to be back.

It was 2003, and I was sitting behind the Oakland A's dugout on the first deck, inhaling the familiar salty fragrance of the San Francisco Bay. I hadn't been inside the Oakland Coliseum in a long time.

At age nine, my blue-eyed daughter, Taylor, was scheduled to throw the ceremonial first pitch in honor of her grandfather—my dad, Carl A. Finley—who passed away on March 30, 2002.

Art Howe introduced himself to Taylor when she entered the field and walked her out to the pitcher's mound. He was speaking softly, and I could tell they were talking about the correct way to hold the ball. He looked a bit surprised when she showed him she knew how.

I could see Taylor's confidence rise in Mr. Howe's presence. She was shy and looked so tiny out on the mound, her long blonde hair restless in the gentle Bay breeze as she positioned herself to wind up, just like Catfish Hunter. I held my breath. She cocked her left knee, aimed her glove at home plate, and tossed the hardball over her head toward the batter's box. Her pitch was true and straight toward the home plate. It fell a foot short, but she looked like a natural. I let out my breath slowly, glad to witness this moment. The next day, Taylor's image appeared on the front page of the *Contra Costa Times*, the *Oakland Tribune*, and the *Tri-Valley Herald*. She had her moment in baseball history, the latest in our Finley family line to do so.

Sitting in that ballpark I had a familiar feeling—that anticipation of what will happen next on that storied baseball field, where almost daily I watched A's legends like Reggie Jackson, Catfish Hunter, Vida Blue, and too many others to name now. I wondered how many baseball games I had attended there. A thousand? The Coliseum felt haunted by the ghosts of my Uncle Charlie and my dad, Carl A. Finley. If they could speak, they would tell a bitter story, a thrilling story, a story about silly things, and secret things. But since they're gone, I'll tell it for them.

It's a story about a baseball team and the men who owned it and steered its destiny for twenty years. It is about me, as well, growing up and coming of age amid the glitter and glory of major league baseball. It is a story untold till now—the Finley side of the story.

All stories have to begin sometime, somewhere. This one starts in the late 1950s with three men, whose lives were previously unconnected.

The first was Charles Oscar Finley, my uncle, who ran a health insurance company in Chicago. The idea for his insurance business had come to him when he was hospitalized for twenty-four months with tuberculosis in the 1940s. By the time he got out his body had withered to ninety-five pounds, but his mind was sharp, and he saw an opportunity. He learned that the doctors did not have a health insurance program designed just for them. He soon offered group insurance to doctors for health and disability, added malpractice to the coverage, and in a few years he was wealthy. Charlie was a great salesman, but otherwise there wasn't anything unusual about him. He was married and had seven children (my cousins). He liked to fish in a pond on his property in La Porte, Indiana. And one of his favorite sports was baseball.

The second man was Arnold Johnson. In 1954 he bought the Philadelphia Athletics and moved the team to Kansas City. Johnson also had financial interests in Yankee Stadium, and he seemed to pay more attention to the Yankees than to the Athletics. In 1959 he made a rare appearance at his team's spring training, where he dropped dead of a cerebral hemorrhage. He left his 52 percent share of the club to his wife and young son. Mrs. Johnson quickly remarried and put the franchise up for auction.

The third man was Ernie Mehl, the sports editor of the *Kansas City Star.* Passionate about bringing Major League Baseball to his city, he had helped Johnson win MLB's approval for the Athletics' move from Philadelphia. Upon Johnson's death Mehl organized a group of Kansas City investors to bid on the team.

My part of the story begins in Dallas. I was a little girl, the only child of Carl and Helen Finley. We were living a Norman Rockwell life in a comfortable one-story brick house with a swing in the backyard. My parents had met while Dad was at Southern Methodist University and Mom was a nurse at Parkland Hospital in Dallas. Both had studied Latin and Greek. They loved history and could recite the entire line of Roman emperors. I have memories of books on ancient Egypt all over the house.

Mom was a medical officer in World War II and made a desperate escape from Corregidor in the Philippines with Douglas MacArthur. Dad worked with the army's Navajo Code Talkers, who devised a code that the Japanese could never break. After the war he studied law, but his interests were academic, and he became the principal at Thomas Jefferson High School, within walking distance of our home. Mom resumed her profession as a nurse at Parkland Hospital.

I would wake in the mornings to the smell of strong coffee. On weekends I would find my parents in the kitchen with the *Dallas Morning News*, working the crossword puzzle and talking of current events. But that was all about to change. Something was going to happen that would throw all of these men and their wives and me into a twenty-year drama that would wreck marriages, tear apart families, rip my dad out of his academic career in Dallas, ruin a writer's dream of owning an MLB team, and pit Charlie against a legion of lesser men who couldn't stand the idea that a mere insurance salesman could waltz in and... well, that's the rest of the story.

It all began on an ordinary Saturday morning with a phone call that changed our lives. Over the next two decades I heard conversations, arguments, lies, and expressions of regret. The players in this drama never noticed me, and I never spoke up. I just held my breath, hoping things would turn out okay.

But now, seeing my daughter out there, I realize that I'm the only one left who can tell this story, and it's time to tell it.

My name is Nancy Finley.

PART I

THE KANSAS CITY ATHLETICS

1960–1968

THE INSURANCE SALESMAN FROM CHICAGO

CHAPTER 1

THE MIDNIGHT MEETING

1961—KANSAS CITY, MISSOURI

The phone rang in the middle of the night.

Wakened from sleep, Crosby Kemper II, president of City National Bank & Trust Company in Kansas City, hung up the receiver and threw on a robe. His twelve-year-old son, Crosby Kemper III, watching from his bedroom window, saw his dad walk down the driveway and get into a car, where his friend and client Charlie O. Finley was waiting. It wasn't the first time Charlie had impulsively roused his banker and confidant in the wee hours to bounce an idea off him. This time it involved a dangerous adversary, Ernie Mehl, the sports editor of the *Kansas City Star*.

BUYING A TEAM AND AN ENEMY

Ernie Mehl had been close to Arnold Johnson before Johnson bought the Philadelphia Athletics in 1954. The team's move to Kansas City, in which Mehl had been instrumental, left him with an obvious conflict of interest as the city's leading sports writer, but he seemed untroubled by it. He continued to advise Johnson about franchise business, trades, and other matters for years, and Johnson apparently took his advice seriously.

The unofficial partnership between Johnson and Mehl was confirmed by cold, hard cash. Mehl and the *Star* requested that Johnson and the Athletics pay the newspaper for the traveling and hotel expenses of its beat reporter Joe McGuff, who followed the team to New York City, Boston, Detroit, and the rest of the American League cities where they played half their schedule. The bill was thousands of dollars each year. Johnson paid.

When the Kansas City baseball franchise was put up for auction after Johnson's sudden death in 1960, Mehl rounded up a group of local investors, fully expecting to acquire the team. When an insurance salesman from Chicago beat him out, he was furious. Charlie Finley had acquired not only a baseball team but also an enemy. Ernest Mehl was once described as a "big, tough, loud, cigar-chomping sports editor,"[1] and he dominated Major League Baseball in Kansas City.

For now, Mehl gave it a chance. He concealed his bitterness over losing the team. In the beginning, the two men enjoyed a brief honeymoon in their relationship. Ernie attended all the games and cheered with everybody else. Just before Charlie stepped for the first time onto the stadium grounds, he and Mehl knew that it was urgent to find a general manager for the team. At Mehl's urging, Charlie hired Mehl's friend Frank Lane. Charlie immediately began innovating, which would eventually get him in trouble with Mehl and others. But he also began courting the fans of Kansas City, and in the beginning Mehl wrote some supportive editorials. The honeymoon, however, was short-lived. Nothing would affect Charlie's time in Kansas City more than the enmity of Ernie Mehl and the *Star*.

STRIPPING THE TEAM

Before Arnold Johnson bought the Athletics, he had owned Yankee Stadium, and his ties to New York franchise remained strong. When he moved the team to Kansas City, he made sure that the owners of the New York Yankees, Del Webb and Dan Topping, were awarded the contract to expand Kansas City's ballpark, which was rechristened Kansas City Municipal Stadium. Construction costs totaled more than $3.2 million and were paid entirely by the city's taxpayers.

Early on, Charlie had heard rumors that Johnson had been stripping the team of its best players and trading them to the Yankees. He hadn't completely believed it, but after he acquired the team he discovered that the rumors were true and that Mehl was complicit. When Johnson moved the team to Kansas City, he had dramatically predicted that they would be a "contender" in five years. But for five years, with Mehl's help, he traded the Athletics' best players to the Yankees, dooming his team to finish at or near the bottom of the standings. There they languished year after year until the new owner eventually turned them around. Charlie immediately announced that there would be no more trades to the Yankees, a decision that could only be seen as a slap at Mehl.

But perhaps the thing that most got Ernie Mehl's goat was that Charlie, unlike Arnold Johnson, had no interest in his advice about how to run the team. His one big concession to Mehl—hiring Frank Lane—ended with Charlie's firing him because he was rude and disrespectful. Mehl would never forgive him for that.

THE END OF PAYOLA

While going through the team's financial records, the new owner came across something that didn't make sense—checks written to Ernie Mehl and Joe McGuff totaling four to five thousand dollars a month. At first, he didn't grasp what they meant. There were no explanatory notations. Charlie took a shot of J&B scotch and looked at them again. Then it hit him: Johnson had been paying the *Star* to write favorable articles about the team.

Charlie had not known of this arrangement when he bought the franchise, so the checks to Mehl and McGuff had stopped when he took over. It must have taken a while for the newspapermen to realize that the payments had come to an end. At some point Mehl broached the subject in conversation with Charlie, who made it clear he had no intention of paying for what in his mind amounted to a journalistic version of a "protection" racket.

"Arnold Johnson paid all travel expenses of Mehl and Joe McGuff," Charlie told the *Star* and other news media. "The books showed it. I was amazed, being a rookie owner, that this was permitted, and when I asked other clubs about such a situation I was told it was not generally done. So I did not permit this to be continued—to me it was nothing but payola."

Next, Charlie tried to assure the fans that he was committed to keeping the Athletics in Kansas City. He had inherited Johnson's lease of Municipal Stadium, which allowed the team to leave if it failed to draw at least 850,000 fans each season. By August 1961, attendance figures were not expected to top seven hundred thousand for the season, and city officials were getting nervous. In front of reporters, Charlie set a piece of paper on fire and said that he was burning the lease, a dramatic gesture to indicate that he wouldn't hold the city to the attendance clause. No one had to worry about losing the team.

Mehl derided the burning of the lease as a "stunt," since it had no legal effect. Burning a document in front of the cameras did not eliminate the attendance clause. Charlie knew that, of course. He was simply trying to send a reassuring message to fans. But Mehl implied it was a trick. After that episode, Charlie's relationship with Mehl, McGuff, and the *Star* steadily declined.

CHARLIE'S HALL OF MIRRORS

The disclosure of the years of "payola" to Mehl explained a lot. Soon after he realized there would be no more bribe money from the Athletics he started bad-mouthing Charlie and, by extension, the team. On August 17, 1961, Mehl wrote a scathing column accusing Charlie of meddling in the decisions of the team manager, Hank Bauer: "He has had to alter his pitching rotation to satisfy the whim of the owner, make line-up changes against his better judgment. He has had his authority usurped...thus making his job all the more difficult."

Mehl also accused Charlie of refusing to promote the team so that falling attendance would give him an excuse to move the Athletics to Dallas: "Had the ownership made a deliberate attempt to sabotage a baseball operation, it could not have succeeded as well." He compared watching Charlie's ownership to "walking through a hall of mirrors, where everything appears to be out of focus. There never has been a baseball operation such as this, nothing so bizarre, so impossibly incongruous." Charlie's management was "incompetent and bizarre," and the owner was a "tyrant" seeking to rob the loyal fans of their team.

The irony here was that the *Star*'s vendetta against Charlie, which poisoned its coverage of the team, was driving attendance down. Mehl and Johnson, not Charlie Finley, consigned the team to the bottom of the standings year after year and betrayed the Athletics' fans.

If Charlie had intended "all along" to take the team out of Kansas City, as Mehl charged, why would he start investing in the franchise's previously neglected farm team? When Charlie took over the team, according to Garrett Smalley, the editor of the *Daily Record and Kansas City Daily News-Press*, Municipal Stadium was "crummy and decaying." Would a man who had a secret plan to move the team spend four hundred thousand dollars of his own money renovating it?

Charlie added fun and attention-getting attractions at Municipal Stadium and promotions like "Farmer's Night," intended to appeal to the city's agricultural bent. He made dozens of speeches around the area promoting the team. If he had plans to move the team, he had an odd way of showing it.

Charlie was furious at Mehl's insinuations. He responded that Mehl had never even asked him to comment on his accusations, and he accused Mehl of demanding kickbacks in exchange for positive press. Mehl and his editor at the *Star*, John W. Colt, denied the accusations.

It was after being vilified by Ernie Mehl in the *Star* that Charlie called for the midnight meeting with the prominent Kansas City banker, Crosby Kemper.

BACK AT THE MIDNIGHT MEETING

And so Crosby Kemper found himself huddled in Charlie Finley's car outside his house in the middle of the night. Charlie told him that he wanted to set Mehl straight, and he wanted to do it in a way that would make the fans understand. In a ceremony at Municipal Stadium, he was going to present the old newsman a "Poison Pen" award.

Kemper was stunned. "Oh, Charlie," he said, shaking his head. "I really don't think you oughta do that. It will be a big mistake. You don't know how influential the *Star* is in this city."

"Crosby," replied Charlie. "I've stood up to bigger men than Ernie Mehl."

"Maybe. But this is Kansas City. It's not your turf. It's theirs."

"We'll see whose turf it is."

"Keep in mind, Charlie, that it was Ahab who ended up impaled on Moby Dick's ass, and not vice versa." Charlie knew what he was talking about—he had seen the movie. But the conversation was over. Charlie had made up his mind. Kemper got out of the car and went back to bed.

It was Charlie's great strength that he almost never backed down from a fight, especially when he thought he was right. It was also his Achilles' heel. If you were a ballplayer who needed a boss in your corner, Charlie's stubbornness was wonderful. But sometimes his battles—even the ones he won—hurt him more than anyone else. In this battle with the most powerful media voice in town, Charlie would land a punch, but the fight proved costly in the end.

THE POISON PEN

Three days after Mehl's August 17 column, the Athletics hosted a doubleheader against the Chicago White Sox. The crowd of nearly ten thousand saw the home team lose the first game. Then a flatbed truck appeared at the far end of the ballpark. As it lumbered across left field, the fans grew quiet. Signs mounted on the sides of the flatbed proclaimed "Ernie Mehl Appreciation Day—Poison Pen Award for 1961" and featured a cartoon image of Mehl working over a typewriter. As the truck circled the field, the stadium organist played "Who's Afraid of the Big Bad Wolf?"

Charlie hoped that the fans would understand that a man who had abused the power of the press had wronged him. But the fans were either indifferent—the strange ceremony drew a confused silence from the crowd—or they sided with Mehl. After all, Charlie had been in Kansas City for only a few months, but Mehl had been a Kansas City reporter for decades. So the public went with the devil they knew over the one they didn't. Charlie's gamble hadn't worked. He failed to win over the public, and he found himself in an all-out war with Ernie Mehl, the most influential figure in sports in Kansas City.

Predictably, there was fallout from the "Poison Pen" incident. The commissioner of Major League Baseball, Ford Frick, called Mehl to apologize personally. True to form, Charlie fought back. First, he convinced Kansas City's mayor pro-tem, Tom Gavin, and several city council members to send a telegram to Frick in support of Charlie. Frick then called Charlie to the commissioner's office to sort out the whole affair. After the meeting, Charlie all but declared victory to the press, telling reporters that Frick in fact had not apologized to Mehl. Frick declined to comment. It would not be Charlie's last public conflict with an MLB commissioner.

When Charlie fired Mehl's friend Frank Lane, Lane returned the favor in an interview with Mehl in the *Kansas City Star*, ripping into Charlie and sharing his opinion that Charlie was thinking of moving the Athletics to Dallas.

Charlie had Lane's replacement lined up. Pat Friday, a thirty-seven-year-old executive from the Chicago insurance office who had been working in the Athletics' front office, would take care of business affairs, while Charlie himself would handle all of the personnel decisions.

Crosby Kemper had been right when he warned Charlie that confronting Mehl in public would backfire, and Charlie knew it. He quickly started working on damage control. Less than a week after the "Poison Pen" ceremony Charlie signed a lease amendment that got rid of the attendance clause once and for all.

CHAPTER 2

A TEAM IS BROUGHT DOWN

1955-1960

DOWN ON THE FARM

Ernie Mehl began preaching the gospel of Kansas City's new baseball team and its owner, Arnold Johnson, in 1954. The *Star* sports editor praised Johnson for plunking down $3.5 million to buy the Athletics. The reality, according to an investigative story in the *Saturday Evening Post*, was somewhat different. Through a series of complex financial maneuvers, Johnson had spent just four hundred thousand dollars to purchase the franchise, and Mehl had promised him that he could "write his own ticket" if he moved the Athletics to Kansas City.

Baseball insiders tended to take a cynical view of Mehl and Johnson. The Chicago White Sox' owner, Bill Veeck, for example, thought that Johnson had moved the Athletics to Kansas City strictly for the short term. Even during the honeymoon period in Kansas City, as Mehl was touting Johnson as the man who made his town "a big-league city," rumors already were flying that Johnson planned to move the Athletics to Los Angeles when his lease expired after the 1959 season. The owner himself added to the suspicion. When a city councilman suggested taxing the Athletics to generate municipal revenue, Johnson threatened to move the team to Southern California after the '57 season, though the prospects for such a move evaporated when the Brooklyn Dodgers moved to Los Angeles in 1958.

Throughout the five years that he owned the Athletics, Johnson, with the tacit approval of Mehl, regularly stripped the team of its best talent and traded them to the Yankees. They made twenty-eight trades with New York, almost all of them lopsidedly in favor of the perennial World Series contenders in the Bronx. It wasn't long before the thrill of being "in the big time of cities," as the *Star* editorialized, faded for Kansas City fans.

In 1957 the Athletics traded Harry Simpson to the Yankees, even though he had been Kansas City's best player the year before. When Simpson struggled the following season, New York just returned him to the Athletics. "It was like a money-back guarantee," wrote a Kansas City columnist years later.

The cozy relationship between the Athletics and the Yankees became embarrassingly obvious. When the Athletics acquired the young slugging prospect Roger Maris in 1957, the American League president, Will Harridge—who had supported Johnson's efforts to buy the Athletics and approved their move to Kansas City—took the unusual step of publicly warning Johnson not to trade Maris to the Yankees for at least eighteen months. Johnson complied, but barely, trading Maris to New York in December 1959. The Athletics got little in return. Batting behind Mantle, Maris's star immediately soared. He was named American League MVP in 1960 and then broke Babe Ruth's single-season home run record the following year in one of pro baseball's most memorable summers.

From 1955 through 1959, while Athletics fans suffered through five straight losing seasons, their best players were shuttled from Kansas City to the Big Apple. Fans and media both started wondering aloud whether Johnson's tight business relationship with Yankees owners Del Webb and Dan Topping was compromising his position as the Athletics' owner.

"Kansas City was not an independent major-league team at all, it was nothing more than a loosely controlled Yankee farm club," Bill Veeck wrote later. He said that he heard the Athletics general manager, Parke Carroll—a former K. C. sports writer—boast openly in baseball meetings that he had nothing to worry about by trading away so many great players because the Yankees' owner, George Weiss, had "promised to take care of" Carroll in return for his help in making those lopsided trades.

As a new decade opened, Athletics fans' enthusiasm was muted. There appeared to be no end in sight to the squad's losing. Then a twist of fate brought about the biggest change of all for Kansas City fans.

In March 1960, the Athletics were in West Palm Beach, Florida, for spring training, and their owner came to watch. The relaxed and optimistic mood of the baseball pre-season was suddenly shattered when Arnold Johnson died of a stroke while driving home from the ballpark. He was fifty-three. After just five seasons in Kansas City, the future of the Athletics again was in doubt.

Ernie Mehl resolved to buy the franchise and keep it in Kansas City. He didn't know, however, that another Midwestern baseball fan wanted to buy the Athletics. From Chicago, Charles Oscar Finley was carefully watching the complicated dealings of Major League Baseball.

THE CALM BEFORE THE STORM

In 1954, the year that Arnold Johnson moved the Philadelphia Athletics to Kansas City, my family was comfortably ensconced in Dallas, unaware that we were about to begin a journey that would end in the trainwreck of the Kansas City Athletics.

My parents were on the move. They settled in the upper-middle-class Walnut Hill neighborhood in north Dallas. Back then Walnut Hill was right out of Norman Rockwell, with parks, swimming pools, and lots of children's activities. Professional men in their early thirties to late forties lived here with their families.

After I was born, Mom quit work. She strove, I think, to have the perfect house and family, or so it appeared. Mom's best friend was Norma Hendrick. I attended the co-op preschool with Norma's daughter Chris, who became my best friend. In 1959, Dad was promoted to principal of Thomas Jefferson High School, three blocks from our home. At thirty-five, he was young for a high school principal, and he already had a master's degree in journalism and was working on his Ph.D. in education. He was well on his way toward his goal of becoming the superintendent of the Dallas Independent School District.

I have memories of Dad in those days walking home from work, dressed in a suit and tie, carrying his briefcase. I would wait outside on the sidewalk until I saw his briefcase swinging in the distance. Then I'd run to him, and the two of us would walk together the rest of the way home. Dad may have been the studious type, but his fathering tended to be lighthearted. He loved playing games and demonstrating magic tricks. He had a big laugh and seldom said "no" to me. Mom, pushed into the role of disciplinarian, would get upset with him over this. I could talk with him, more so than with my mother. In the way that young girls often are, I was somewhat smitten by Dad. I sort of remember (and am told) I used to tell Dad that I wanted to marry him when I grew up.

Those were idyllic years for me, the most innocent time of my childhood, living in the cocoon that was Walnut Hill. Mom and Dad seemed happy. I was happy. Then one lovely Saturday morning the phone rang. It was Uncle Charlie.

He had called before. He and Dad were close, and despite the marked differences in their personalities—or perhaps because of them—they got along well. Charlie wanted to know if Dad was interested in working for him with the baseball team. Charlie needed someone he could trust to help run the franchise. The catch was that Dad would have to move his family to Kansas City. Dad politely declined. It was a flattering offer, but he was rising quickly in the Dallas public schools, and he and his wife and young daughter would stay where they were.

The calendar said the '50s had ended, but in our tranquil neck of the woods, there was no sign that the new decade would be much different.

We didn't know it, but our family had just boarded a train for Kansas City, and the tranquility of Walnut Hill was coming to an end.

CHAPTER 3

NOT INVITED
TO THE DANCE

1960

Soon after Arnold Johnson died, his family put his baseball team up for auction. Ernie Mehl hurriedly put together a group of Kansas City businessmen to pool their assets to purchase the team, expecting to become in due course the majority owner of the Athletics.

By the late 1950s, baseball owners formed an exclusive club of old-money boys and *nouveau riche* businessmen, and they looked out for each other. Charlie was a self-made millionaire, but he was just an insurance salesman—not part of the club. When it became clear that Charlie might actually acquire the Athletics in 1960, the other owners assigned the Baltimore Orioles' chairman, Joe Iglehart, to investigate him. Iglehart reported back to the owners: "Under no conditions should this person be allowed into our league."

The owners didn't take the warning seriously, but people in Kansas City worried that the newcomer would move the Athletics out of town, so Mehl and local restaurateur J. W. ("Jud") Putsch were appointed as co-chairmen of a committee to find local investors. Just six years after

Mehl and the *Kansas City Star* had successfully backed Johnson in bringing the Athletics to town, Mehl had to fight the battle all over again. He
felt that they were his team, and everybody knew it. No one had done
more than Mehl to sell tickets and cultivate interest in the Kansas City
Athletics during the team's first half-decade in town.

So to save the baseball tradition he had started, Mehl went back to
work. By the end of June 1960, Putsch and Mehl had recruited nine local
businessmen willing to put up two hundred thousand dollars each, for
a total of $1.8 million, and Mehl reported that there were additional
individuals and groups inside and outside Kansas City who were interested in purchasing the team.

He did even more. With attendance figures down in mid-June by
about a hundred thousand from the previous year, Mehl launched a
citywide ticket-buying drive, led by the *Star*, which bought twenty-five
thousand tickets. Meanwhile, ownership groups wanting to move the
Athletics to New Jersey, St. Louis, and several other cities started raising
money.

Overseeing the sale of the team was Judge Robert J. Dunne of the
probate court, who excluded Charlie and other prospective owners and
narrowed the field of competitors to two—Mehl's Kansas City group
and a St. Louis syndicate led by the investment banker Elliot Stein. On
November 15, Dunne awarded the Athletics to Stein, but the deal fell
through three days later, and the team went back into probate court.
This time Charlie made the cut, and he began bidding against Mehl's
Kansas City group. At one point Mehl was certain he had won the auction and was said to have been celebrating with his associates, but seemingly out of nowhere Charlie appeared again and raised his bid to
$1,975,000. The Kansas City investors finally bowed out on December
19. Within two months, Charlie exercised his option on the remaining
interests for an additional $1.9 million. He had snatched the prize from
under Mehl's nose, and for the first time since the Athletics had come to
town, the team owner would not be beholden to Ernie Mehl or the *Kansas City Star*. For Athletics' fans, news of a new owner wasn't so bad. A

little change might free the team from the Yankees' clutches and bring it out of the cellar.

At first Mehl was in shock. Still, he knew no reason he couldn't manipulate Charlie as he had manipulated Johnson. Surely he could handle the ingénue insurance salesman, and the party would go on.

BANKING ON KEMPER

UMB Financial Services, one of the biggest banks in the nation, was founded as City Center Bank in Kansas City. William T. Kemper bought the bank in 1913, and in 1919 his son Rufus Crosby Kemper became the president, a position he held until his son, R. Crosby Kemper Jr., replaced him in 1959.

A year after taking the helm of UMB, Kemper Jr. joined other city business leaders at a Chamber of Commerce luncheon celebrating the new owner of the Kansas City Athletics, Charles Oscar Finley, whose popularity was sealed when he assured fans that he would not move the team. Kemper was seated right next to Charlie, and the two men hit it off right away, starting a lasting friendship.

During their luncheon conversation, Kemper asked Charlie which bank had financed his purchase of the Athletics, which cost nearly four million dollars. Charlie's answer stunned him: "Well, I actually haven't lined up financing yet." Trying not to look too surprised, Kemper offered to finance the deal. Charlie agreed, without hesitation. The sale of the Kansas City Athletics was thus finalized on little more than a handshake and a smile between two businessmen who had never before met.

Being new to town, Charlie looked to Kemper for advice on how things were done in Kansas City. "Charlie never took the advice," recalls Kemper's son, Crosby Kemper III, with a chuckle, "but he'd ask for it."

Kemper learned that being Charlie Finley's banker meant keeping unusual hours. Charlie often would call late at night, sometimes even after midnight on a weeknight, to talk business. Kemper III remembers the phone ringing in the wee hours when he was a young child. His dad

would head outside in a robe and slippers and sit in the passenger seat of
Charlie's car, discussing whatever was on Charlie's mind.

While Charlie liked to do business on the fly, the Kempers were
cautious and meticulous. The financing for Charlie's purchase of the
Athletics was the biggest loan they had ever made. Charlie's insurance
company and holding company had nearly identical names, and Kemper placed the collateral for the deal under the wrong company in the
contract. So he had to drive from Kansas City to Charlie's ranch in
LaPorte, Indiana—an eleven-hundred-mile round trip—in the middle
of the night to get Charlie's signature on the amended contract.

Now in his mid-sixties, R. Crosby Kemper III remembers Charlie as
a kind and loyal friend to his father. He also recalls Charlie's intensity,
which made him occasionally "unheedful to his surroundings. When he
was into something he was *really* into something." Kemper's childhood
image of Charlie was that of a showman with natural charisma, white
hair, and a long cherubic face.

"There was something genie-like about him," Kemper says. "It's like
there was a force field around him, something magical. I always felt like
I was in the presence of P. T. Barnum; he was an awe-inspiring figure,
like a magician or the master of ceremonies of a three-ring circus. You
always expected him to produce something you'd never seen before; he
wasn't distant or cold, he existed in a kind of separate zone. I didn't feel
warmth emanating from him, but I liked being around him. He was fun
to watch, always animated, you could just feel his energy." A *Life* magazine article about Charlie noted his "erect and jaunty carriage, white
hair, a classic profile, heavy dark brows, and burning brown eyes."

Charlie's energy was on display during his honeymoon with Kansas
City fans in the early months of 1961. He spoke at 125 civic and business
clubs, talking up his determination to give the doormat team new life.
He admired the work ethic and the witty, offbeat promotions of Bill
Veeck, whose fan-friendly baseball stunts were fun and unpretentious
and displayed a flair for theatrics—and the absurd. Veeck is best known
for the time in 1951 he sent a midget named Eddie Gaedel up to bat. To
baseball's stodgy and conservative owners, promotional antics were

affronts to the game's dignity. The old guard of baseball disliked Veeck, and they would dislike Charlie.

BURNING THE BUS

It was clear from the very first game at Municipal Stadium under Charlie's ownership that he wouldn't be part of the old guard. Ernie Mehl, sitting in the upper stands, had no intimation of what was coming.

The fans were chatting, sipping beer, and waiting for the game to start. Suddenly, they grew quiet. They watched as a beat-up old shuttle bus lumbered onto left field. Exchanging perplexed glances, they wondered what was going on. Then Frank Lane walked out to the bus and splashed it with gasoline. An instant later it was engulfed in black and orange flames. Then an unfamiliar voice came over the loudspeaker. It was the team's new owner. Charlie introduced himself and explained that the burning of the bus was his way of announcing that the days of shuttling Kansas City's best talent to the Bronx were over. The Athletics would no longer be the Yankees' farm team. After a pause, a few fans started clapping, and soon the stadium was filled with applause and shouts of approval. Charlie grinned from ear to ear.

Ernie Mehl, of course, didn't miss the subtle jab at himself and Al Johnson, and like the bus, he smoldered as he watched from the stands.

Charlie was just getting started. He installed a petting zoo behind the right field fence, where a flock of sheep now grazed. The animals were dyed different colors—green, yellow, orange, blue, purple, and pink—and were watched over by a "shepherd" who looked like something out of a Christmas pageant. They were joined by capuchin monkeys in cages, each named after one of my uncles—as in, "I'll be a monkey's uncle." Another one was named after my grandfather. Peacocks roamed the grounds—Charlie loved those birds, with their brightly iridescent plumage—and pheasants and rabbits completed the menagerie.

Charlie thought Municipal Stadium was rather drab, so as part of his four-hundred-thousand-dollar renovation, he painted the box seats "citrus yellow," the reserved and bleacher seats "desert turquoise," and the foul poles fluorescent pink. Then he sandblasted a wall outside the stadium and painted it yellow. He added 1,200 seats in the left-field bleachers, built a picnic area behind those seats shaded by sugar maple trees, piped radio broadcasts of games into the restrooms, installed fluorescent lights in the dugouts so fans could see the players and the manager during night games, and lit up the exterior of the ballpark.

Municipal Stadium became even more colorful at Easter, when the Finley men, dressed up as rabbits, handed out candy to young fans. Then there was "Harvey," the mechanical rabbit with flashing red eyes that would rise up out of the grass to the right of home plate to deliver a fresh baseball to the umpire whenever he needed it. As it rose from the ground with a loud ascending whistle, the organist played "Here Comes Peter Cottontail." A descending whistle accompanied Harvey's return to his subterranean home. A few opposing team batters have been startled by the Harvey's sudden emergence from the ground, and one batter jumped a foot in the air the first time he experienced Harvey.

Another innovation at home plate was "Little Blowhard," an automated device that blew dirt off of the plate, a task otherwise performed by the umpire with a whisk broom.

Charlie was the first to use an electric scoreboard to deliver interesting information about the game and individual players—he called them "Fan-a-Grams." Today, it's standard procedure for scoreboards to communicate more than the box score, but Charlie started it all fifty years ago.

No one in baseball had ever done these things at a Major League Ballpark. They revealed the little kid in Charlie—the wide-eyed, fun-loving boy who got a kick out of the smallest things. Charlie saw baseball and entertainment through the eyes of a little boy. "Today's children are tomorrow's fans," he explained.

A CHICAGO SERENADE

The night of December 19, 1960, was cold in Chicago, but the strains of Frank York's Strolling Violins gave a warm glow to the Porterhouse

Room of the Hotel Sherman in the Loop. Just as the maestro was cuing his players for their next number, in walked a group of chilled but happy men, led by Charlie Finley, the new owner of the Kansas City Athletics baseball club.

The musicians quickly regrouped, and a few minutes later they serenaded Charlie's party with Rodgers and Hammerstein's "Everything's Up to Date in Kansas City." Transforming his string ensemble into a Dixieland band, York followed up with a jazzy version of the "Missouri Waltz."

Charlie was so enthusiastic about York's renditions of these songs that he asked him to record them for the baseball fans of Kansas City. Two weeks later, Charlie had his "Official Theme Song of the Kansas City Athletics."

ROMANCING KANSAS CITY

Writing in *Sports Illustrated* in the summer of 1961, Rex Lardner described Charlie's efforts "to charm reluctant Kansas City fans." Those efforts seemed to be paying off in that first year. Kansas City Mayor Roe Bartle gushed that "Finley has put more spirit into the city than anyone in the past decade. He holds the heart of Kansas City in the palm of his hand."

Lardner reported that Charlie was paying attention to the players as well, taking them out to expensive restaurants, giving them gifts, and entertaining them and their families at his home. "He wants a happy team…and he has shown himself to be the kindliest owner in baseball." Charlie seemed to be winning everyone's heart. "It is doubtful," Lardner wrote, "if any owner or part owner has ever been so solicitous about the comfort of the fan or the peace of mind of the players."

That first year, Charlie poured his heart and soul into the team. At the urging of Ernie Mehl, he hired as general manager Frank Lane at the highest salary ever paid for a G. M. But signs of trouble emerged early on. "Lane thinks Finley's solicitude toward the team is absurd," wrote Lardner. When Charlie announced that there would be no more trades to the Yankees (and emphasized the point with the burning bus), Lane publicly responded that, to the contrary, he would make deals with the Yankees or any ball club if he felt it would help the team. Charlie overruled some of Lane's trades, which surely rankled.

All honeymoons come to an end, some sooner rather than later.

CHAPTER 4

KANSAS CITY, HERE WE ARE

1961

FRIENDLY PERSUASION

Charlie needed someone on the ground in Kansas City right away to look after his baseball interests—someone he could trust. In 1961 he brought in his brother, Fred Finley, to handle the club's promotions, but that didn't work out.

In the fall of 1961, Charlie started romancing Dad. It began with that Saturday morning phone call. Soon, however, he started calling Dad every week to say that a roundtrip airline ticket on Braniff Airlines had been purchased for him to come up to Kansas City on a Friday night and return to Dallas on Sunday. To Mom's chagrin, Dad began traveling there on weekends, the only days he had off from his responsibilities at Thomas Jefferson High School. Once he began traveling, my parents' bridge parties stopped.

As Dad's travel increased, I missed him more and more. It felt to me as though we practically lived at Love Field. I kept his picture with me and cried every time after we returned home from driving him to the airport for another flight to Kansas City.

To maintain family time, Mom and I began to visit Kansas City two weekends a month. Sometimes we traveled by train, which I enjoyed. Whenever we flew, it was always on Braniff. I liked Braniff because its planes were yellow, orange, lime green, or blue. The stewardesses wore uniforms that matched the color of the plane. If the aircraft was blue, they all wore blue. But Braniff's use of color was fairly pale compared with what Uncle Charlie would do in Kansas City.

When I first laid eyes on Kansas City Municipal Stadium, I was just four years old. It was the perfect age to be enthralled by the bizarre attractions behind the outfield walls. While Mom and Charlie's wife, Aunt Shirley, visited, my cousins and I made the ballpark our playground. David, Uncle Charlie's and Aunt Shirley's youngest son, was my age, and we loved roaming the grounds together.

Baseball had never been a big part of our lives—Mom was not a fan and I was more interested in my stuffed animals than in a team whose logo was an elephant. But now Dad was increasingly involved with what was going on in Kansas City, which, it turned out, involved much more than the game of baseball. In Dallas, my parents had always seemed to get along well, but Dad's work in Kansas City created tension in their relationship.

The first argument over the Athletics I heard between my parents took place when Dad came home from Kansas City with an eight-by-ten photograph of a blonde woman signed by "Cricket Blake." Cricket was the role that Connie Stevens played in the television series *Hawaiian Eye*. When the starlet visited Kansas City, Charlie had asked Dad to show her around Municipal Stadium. Dad didn't realize that the autographed photo would make Mom angry. It would not be the last argument that baseball sparked between my parents.

All through 1962, Charlie pleaded with Dad to move to Kansas City, going so far as to promise he would buy our family a home there. Charlie had always heard his parents brag about Dad's intellectual powers and his education. I believe this is why Charlie wanted Dad in Kansas

City so badly—he knew Dad would understand the business and legal ends of the business. He also would watch Charlie's back.

At the same time, Charlie, who never went to college, was jealous of Dad's academic success. He must have grown tired of hearing his own father hold up Dad as the ideal son. I heard that as a child Charlie had a speech impediment, which is why he spoke slowly at times. Years later, when he owned the Athletics, sports writers mistook his deliberate and careful way of talking for arrogance or condescension.

Charlie applied his powerful salesmanship on Dad, but Dad held out, refusing to commit to the Athletics full-time. The lingering job offer divided our close-knit extended Finley family. Everyone seemed to have an opinion. Grandmother Finley begged Dad to refuse Uncle Charlie's offer. Mom was against it, too, anticipating how uncomfortable she would feel in the world of sports and entertainment. Granddad, however, urged Dad to join his favorite nephew and accept the offer.

Dad held out for nearly a year, but Charlie eventually wore him down. He walked away from the career he loved for an uncertain life in professional baseball. In the summer of 1963, Dad put our Texas house up for sale.

Mom began to pack for the move to Kansas City. She said good-bye to Norma Hendrick, her best friend and neighbor, and I said good-bye to Chris. I was saddened by the idea that I would not be able to visit my Finley grandparents and cousins regularly. I worried that my cousin Tommy might forget what I looked like. As things turned out, that would be the least of my worries in Kansas City.

A HANDS-ON OWNER

Uncle Charlie went to West Palm Beach in early 1961 for his first spring training game as owner of the Kansas City Athletics. Almost from the beginning, Charlie got involved with the general manager's duties, making many of the personnel decisions. And he was good at it. It took a while for his best decisions to pay off, but for a man who had never played professional baseball, he became quite good at judging who possessed the ability to be a Major League star and who didn't. Nevertheless, Charlie's hands-on style was difficult for the team's general managers and managers, and he went through many front-office men over the years.

That first season in Kansas City set the tone. Charlie's Athletics began the year with Joe Gordon as manager and Frank Lane as general manager. Before season's end, Gordon and Lane were gone.

And something else would be gone, as well—the selfish, hypocritical, and cruel grip of the sports media clique that had trapped the franchise in failure. And thus began the long sail back to greatness.

But headwinds were rising.

CHAPTER 5

LIFE AT THE MUEHLEBACH

1963

A s a five-year-old girl enthralled with her new surroundings, I was having a wonderful time, especially at the ballgames at Municipal Stadium, an exciting place where we were expected to socialize with fans. One of the most dedicated Athletics fans was Harry S. Truman, the former president and, like Dad and Charlie, a thirty-second-degree Mason. He came to almost every A's home game. Mom, Dad, and I often visited with him, and I remember sitting in his lap during a game. Once he gave me a box of lollipops, which I handed out after the game to anyone we came across: stadium ushers, the Muehlebach Hotel bellboy, the elevator operator, and our housekeeper.

Away from the ballpark, Charlie's suite at the Muehlebach Hotel was the center of his world whenever he came to Kansas City. It was where he conducted business for his thriving Chicago insurance firm, where he negotiated contracts with ballplayers itching for a tiny raise, and where he hosted his well-attended postgame parties. Mom, Dad, and I would get to know the hotel quite well.

Though I didn't appreciate it at the time, Muehlebach was the biggest and best hotel in town, a symbol of old Kansas City. Built in 1915 by George Muehlebach, who inherited and expanded his father's brewing empire, the stately twelve-story hotel has hosted presidents and celebrities, and it was home to Carl and Helen Finley and me when we arrived in Kansas City in August 1963. After our suburban ranch-style house in Texas, I found hotel living fascinating at first. The beds came out of the wall!

Compared with Dallas, Kansas City was one big party. We'd often visit Uncle Charlie's spacious suite, which was always filled with people. I remember lots of food. While I walked around, Mom would sit with Aunt Shirley, who had sparkly blue eyes and always smiled. My earliest memory of Uncle Charlie is his bushy eyebrows and commanding presence. He would say, "Come to Uncle Charlie!" But I'd hide behind Mom. At age four, I was afraid of large voices, though once I was a little older, it didn't bother me.

Once, before a game began I discovered I could dance on the dugout. Dad was furious. He was afraid a foul ball might hit me. He told me never to do that again.

Our "neighbors" at the Muehlebach were always changing. And there was a man in a suit, the bellhop, who stood in the elevator and pressed the button for you! I remember being afraid the rickety old thing would stop between floors and we'd be stuck. The hotel seemed dark inside, and busy...full of men with cigars and pretty women.

But life at the Muehlebach soon turned boring for me. There was no backyard, so I could not play outside anymore. I missed my friend Christine, and until kindergarten began the following month, I had no chance to make new friends who were my age. My best companion was my stuffed Cecil the Seasick Sea Serpent, from a popular kids' show, *Beanie and Cecil*. We were supposed to stay at the hotel for just a week or two before moving into the home that Charlie had promised that he would buy for Dad. We ended up staying at the Muehlebach for eight months.

Even though Dad and Charlie were buddies, our extended hotel stay was Dad's first lesson that when Charlie promised you something, you had to stay on him constantly to get him to deliver. Mom, more anxious every day to get back to a normal life, frequently reminded Dad of Charlie's promise.

As an incentive to leave his career in education, Charlie had given Dad a minority ownership in the franchise, and he assumed his first position with the Athletics, in the public relations department, before the 1963 season. Later that year, his title became team business manager, and before long, he became the key member of the front office, performing a wide range of jobs.

For Mom and me, the stadium became the lone bright spot in our lives. We would go there for almost every home game. From our seats just behind the dugout, always on the first base side, I could see other kids sitting in the stands and I wished I could get to know them. Our outings became a family affair, since Mom and Aunt Shirley were good friends and always sat together at the ballpark.

There I discovered Harvey the Mechanical Rabbit, who rose out of the ground behind the home plate umpire and provided him with a fresh baseball. When he popped up, Harvey's glowing eyes were flashing red. I found that terrifying and had to hide my face when he appeared.

Ever the pragmatist, Aunt Shirley made Kansas City her second home. She was more relaxed about the world of professional baseball and its quirks than my mother was. Maybe Shirley was more flexible because of her many children, or maybe because of the unpredictable nature of her husband. Either way, Mom admired her for it.

While the games were fun, postgame events were something different altogether. People called Kansas City "Cow Town," but Charlie's postgame parties in his suite at the Muehlebach belied that dull and backward image. Mom did not care for these glamorous, sometimes boozy soirées, which drew a much faster crowd than she was accustomed to—ballplayers, front-office employees, business leaders, the occasional Hollywood celebrity, such as Marie McDonald and Connie Stevens, along with a Missouri beauty queen or two, and always a Miss America. And this being Kansas City, local mobsters sometimes attended these parties, which only added to Mom's anxiety.

In 1963, Kansas City wasn't as nearly corrupt as it had been during Prohibition, when Tom Pendergast and Johnny Lazia had a stranglehold on the city. The federal government had since cleaned up a lot of this. But in some ways, new mobster faces had merely replaced the old ones, and "the Outfit"—as Kansas City mafiosi were called in the '60s—was alive and well. Nick Civella ran the city's organized crime at this time. After just a short time in Kansas City, Mom and Dad soon learned how entrenched the mob was, and had always been, in the seemingly quiet midwestern city. Mom was alarmed, but Dad was amused. And when Mom realized they were socializing with a mobster or two at Charlie's postgame parties, she went straight home, leaving Dad to enjoy the party. The network of Mehl, the Yankees, and Johnson had not been connected to the Kansas City mob, which never exercised control over the baseball team.

My mom and Shirley were scheduled to host a dinner for the Trumans in Kansas City, when suddenly Shirley was called to the bedside of her ailing mother in Chicago. Shirley told mom she was sure she could handle it by herself. A childhood spent picking cotton on the family farm on Mexia, Texas, may have taught Mom self-reliance, but it had not prepared her to host a dinner for a former president and first lady. Mom was never so nervous; she could barely remember which sides of the plate the fork and knife went on. Despite her crash course in high-level hospitality, the dinner came off without a hitch.

Our baseball home was fun, exotic, and carefree. Nobody realized it yet, but my home in Kansas City would be anything but.

CHAPTER 6

WHAT COLOR IS SECOND BASE?

1963

W hile Dad and Pat Friday and I were sitting in the Muehlebach lounge, Charlie popped in. "I've got the best-looking uniforms you've ever seen," he excitedly said.

He went in the back of his suite, and returned with the loudest, most brightly colored uniforms that Dad had ever seen. Dad grinned and said "Beautiful!" Pat Friday whispered in Dad's ear, "God awful."

Dad said he liked the new colors. The baseball establishment did not.

Uniforms had been the same color in the major leagues for at least sixty years. The home team wore white, and the road team wore gray. The one exception was the Yankees, who wore their famous pinstripes over their white home jersey.

Now there was a new exception. The Kansas City Athletics' main color was gold—"Fort Knox gold," to be precise—save for the hat, undershirt, and stirrups, which now were "kelly green." Within a year, another color, "wedding gown white," was added.

Early in the season, Athletics' right fielder Gino Cimoli passed a few opposing players who snickered at his uniforms, and he half-jokingly warned them, "Don't even say a word."

Predictably, baseball's old guard didn't care for the uniforms. The New York Yankees gave a public thumbs-down to the bright uniform colors. At the 1963 All-Star Game, the American League squad manager Ralph Houk—also the Yankees manager—refused to play the Athletics' lone All-Star because he felt the new green-and-gold uniforms were so undignified as to be beneath the game.

Paul Lukas, who writes about uniforms for ESPN.com and UniWatchBlog.com, says that time has vindicated Charlie, praising him for "dragging baseball kicking and screaming into the modern age." It's undeniable that he was an eccentric maverick. But he wasn't trying to be different just for the hell of it. There was a business motivation, too; usually a forward-thinking reason tied to the changing times. In the early 1960s, color television sales were on the rise, and Charlie "was the first to see color TV in terms of the changing color palette in baseball," Lukas writes. He knew that his bright uniforms would stand out on those new color sets.

Charlie also was one of the first to add players' last names to team uniforms. True to form, he didn't stop there. He started putting players' nicknames on the back of the uniforms until baseball officials made him stop. Charlie understood that increased TV coverage brought players closer to fans, and names on the jerseys helped television viewers to identify players. "He rocked the boat in all kinds of ways," says Lukas. "In retrospect, Finley did a lot of things that were cool."

A year after the new uniforms were introduced, Charlie added white shoes—"albino kangaroo white." More than forty-five seasons later, despite all of the changes in baseball over the years, the white shoes remain a part of Athletics baseball tradition.

SYNESTHESIA

There's no denying that Charlie was a visionary, but there might have been more behind the colorful uniforms than his ability to predict the influence of color television. Charlie was always fascinated with color, especially bright colors, and years later I finally found out why.

In 2004, my ten-year-old daughter Taylor wrote a letter to the editor of our local newspaper about a controversy surrounding the Pledge of Allegiance. Her letter concluded, "I see a yellow side to life in the corner of my eyes. I see America." When her father and I chuckled over this quirky remark, she turned to us and asked, "When you hear a number, do you see a color?" Her father and I both said, "No." In time, we learned that the association in her mind of numbers or letters with particular colors is real and is a form of a neurological phenomenon called synesthesia. It is thought to have a strong genetic component and is the subject of intense study in the cognitive sciences.

When I first read about synesthesia, I looked up and noticed the orange Athletics baseball displayed in our home. Next to this orange baseball was a group photograph of our 1973 team, decked out in green and gold. Suddenly it hit me—*Charlie had synesthesia!*

SEEING THE GAME IN 3-D

Charlie, like Taylor, must have inherited this from somewhere in the Finley family tree. Now so much made sense—the colored sheep with their shepherd in his multi-colored robe, the brightly painted walls inside Municipal Stadium, the peacocks, the brightly colored uniforms, the green bats.

As I learned more about synesthesia in connection with my daughter, I began to understand that Charlie's synesthesia may explain a whole lot more than merely his fascination with colors. In synesthete brains, there are often cross-connections between different senses, producing unusual associations between numbers, words, physical sensations, emotions, and visual experiences. This connectivity has been described by one psychologist as an exaggerated version of the "cross-talk present in all brains."

How could an insurance salesman put together a baseball team that could win three consecutive World Series, at a time, moreover, when automated statistical analysis (as in *Moneyball*) did not exist?

My husband, Morgan, believes Charlie viewed the game not in terms of statistics but in three dimensions, like three-dimensional chess. Morgan used to wonder how Charlie, sitting in his office in Chicago and unable to see the field, could place a phone call in the middle of a game and insert a certain player into a certain position at a certain time and have it work. "Charlie could look over the field in his mind's eye like a chess player who scans the whole board, and simply *feels* what needs to be done. Logic has little to do with it. It is intuitive, almost subconscious."

Typically, when Charlie placed such a call, he had been *listening* to the game, not *watching* it. During most of the regular season in Oakland, Charlie remained in his office in Chicago. My mother, at home in Kansas City, would hold the phone receiver up to the radio, and Charlie, on the other end of the call, would listen to the game play-by-play over the phone. Every so often, he would select another line on his office phone and call the Oakland office. Those dreaded calls from Charlie!

"Perhaps," said Morgan, "he could still see the field in his mind."

Digging deeper into recent research on synesthesia, I came across the following passage (my italics) that was like a lightning strike in a dark sky:

> Beyond the vague assertion that synesthesia might enhance sensory and intersensory processing...*can synesthesia actually enhance sophisticated and abstract mental abilities?* Ramachandran and Hubbard pointed out that many synesthetes with *visual-spatial* number forms claimed such enhancement did occur.

Visual-spatial? You mean like imagining a baseball game being played? I continued reading:

> When a number-form synesthete imagines or visualizes a number in front of him he always sees it occupying a specific location in space; the numbers are arranged sequentially along

a number line that can be highly convoluted *in three dimen-sions—sometimes even doubling back on itself.*

Intriguingly some of them reported being able to "see hidden relationships" from unusual vantage points geometrically as a result of the numerical landscape....[1]

The more I learned about synesthesia, the more it seemed to explain about Charlie. When he chose green and gold for the team's colors, he probably saw his team in those colors. Perhaps he saw the word "baseball" as gold and green. He didn't choose those colors because they were outlandish. Quite simply, he couldn't help it.

And as for what my husband said about Charlie's seeing the diamond in three dimensions, many synesthetes "can mentally take on different perspectives, 'zooming in and out' or 'moving around' the form."[2] Listening to the play-by-play broadcast in Chicago, did Charlie see colors in his head? Did he see a three-dimensional baseball field? Did he see that the pieces on the infield were not positioned well for the situation of the moment? What did he see when he picked up the phone to call Dad, quickly, before the next batter came up? Many people have called Charlie a genius, but I wonder if he was something else—what you might call a "sports savant."

A RESTLESS OWNER

Charlie changed more than the uniforms. After one and a half seasons, he replaced Hank Bauer as manager with Ed Lopat, who led the Athletics for the 1963 season and then was fired himself. Mel McGaha replaced him before the 1964 campaign. The Athletics kept losing. And they kept losing fans. Attendance had dropped to 762,000 fans for the '63 season, and Kansas City leaders were not doing much to help the team.

Charlie was growing frustrated. And getting restless.

CHAPTER 7

DRAMA WITH THE CITY COUNCIL

1963

C harlie was not having much fun.

The end of the 1963 season, his third as owner, was when his relationship with Kansas City started to unravel. He was expected to sign a new lease for Municipal Stadium in January 1964. Charlie and the Athletics were paying half a million dollars a year in rent to the city, and the end-of-season negotiations with the city council weren't going well.

Ernie Mehl and the *Kansas City Star* continued to hammer Charlie, printing rumors that he had begun talking to Dallas, Louisville, Oakland, and other cities about moving the team. Mehl, of course, coyly refrained from mentioning that his late pal Arnold Johnson had tried to do that for years before the Finley era, with Mehl's acquiescence.

Contrary to what Mehl was writing, Charlie was eager to work out a deal to keep the franchise in Kansas City. After all, he had spent hundreds of thousands of dollars less than three years earlier to improve the city's ballpark.

After the November 1963 elections, the lame-duck members of the city council met with Charlie, who was demanding a two-year lease rather than a four-year lease. He had threatened to take the team to Louisville, Kentucky, but the owners blocked the move and gave Charlie until February 1, 1964, to sign a new lease in Kansas City. After marathon negotiating sessions, Charlie and the city council finally reached an agreement. With the Athletics' lease on Muni Stadium extended for four years, the city fathers and the fans were euphoric. Charlie was excited, happy, and relieved not to have to think about moving the team. It seemed that the Kansas City Athletics were entering a new era.

Then Charlie discovered that the Chiefs, the American Football League franchise newly arrived in Kansas City from Dallas, were paying just one dollar per season to play at Municipal Stadium—the stadium Charlie had paid hundreds of thousands of dollars out of his own pocket to renovate. Now Charlie was furious. The relationship between Kansas City and the A's office was at an all-time low. Charlie wanted to keep the team there, but did Kansas City want them?

SATCHEL PAIGE

The home of one of the Negro leagues' most famous teams, the Monarchs, Kansas City had a rich history of Negro baseball. In 1965, Charlie paid tribute to those great Negro league teams when he signed the fifty-nine-year-old Satchel Paige, a former Monarch pitcher, to play one game for the Athletics, an otherwise meaningless late-season contest against the Boston Red Sox. Paige had been Major League Baseball's oldest rookie when Bill Veeck signed him to the Cleveland Browns in 1948. He followed Veeck to the hapless St. Louis Browns in 1951, retiring after three seasons there at the age of forty-seven.

Charlie invited several Negro league veterans, including Cool Papa Bell, to the game with Paige, introducing them before the game to the crowd of only ten thousand. Paige, "for effect," was perched on a rocking chair in the bullpen, attended by a "nurse" between innings.

Paige pitched amazingly well, tossing three shutout innings. He took the mound at the top of the fourth, when, on cue, manager Haywood Sullivan replaced him with Diego Segui. Paige walked off the field to a warm ovation with a one-to-nothing lead. The lights dimmed, and led by the announcer, the fans lit matches and cigarette lighters and sang "The Old Gray Mare."

The Athletics lost five to two, but nobody remembers that. The unforgettable night—a tribute to the promotional genius of Uncle Charlie—was hard to square with the suspicion that the owner was itching to move the ball club.

CHAPTER 8

OVERLAND PARK

1964

F our years into their quarrel, Ernie Mehl liked to harass Charlie with a special weapon: the Associated Press. Newspapers around the country that otherwise never would have bothered with Charlie or the Athletics ran Mehl's articles right off the AP wire. And these articles always put Charlie in a bad light.

On May 23, 1964, a San Antonio newspaper ran an AP story headlined "Another Setback for Finley & the A's." The incident that occasioned the article was trivial—the city had prevented Charlie from shooting off fireworks after home runs—but the headline contributed to Mehl's campaign to brand Charlie as a loser.

MOVING WITH THE MOB

When Uncle Charlie was wooing Dad to join the Athletics' front office, he promised that he would buy us a house when we moved to Kansas City. But once we made the move, that promise seemed to be forgotten. The months passed, and to Mom's dismay we still had no house, camping amid uncertainty and consternation at the Meuhlebach Hotel.

In early 1964, we made a move on our own. We left the hotel and rented a home in the Hyde Park district. We lived on Janssen Place, a wide, picturesque street with a gated entry in the heart of Kansas City. Bisected by a grass island in the middle, the street was dotted with beautiful mansions on both sides. Three of the large homes had been converted into duplexes, one of which we rented. At the other end of Janssen Place was that rarity in Kansas City—a hill, which we used in the winter for sledding.

The move, which took place on a snowy day in January, did nothing to reassure my mother about Kansas City. I was at school. Dad left work early, picked up Mom at the hotel for the last time, and headed out to Janssen Place. They met two young movers, who brought in our stove, ice box, and dining room furniture. Mom noticed a third man—handsome, dark-haired, and dressed in white coveralls. He caught her attention mostly because he never lifted a finger to help the other two movers. Instead, he sat at the table chatting with Mom and Dad and sipping coffee. His name was George. "He seemed amazed and so happy to meet me," Mom recalled many years later.

After the movers had left, Dad told Mom the punch line about their chatty visitor. George was a mobster, he said with amusement—the second-highest mafia "don" in Kansas City. A few years later, Dad told me that he knew people in Kansas City who would professionally "assassinate" someone. I don't think he was joking, and he said he never told anyone else about it.

A HOME OF OUR OWN

More than a year after we had left Dallas and nine months after we had moved to Janssen Place, Charlie finally made good on his promise to buy us a house. We were delighted to move into a suburban ranch-style home like the one we'd left in Dallas. It was in a pretty, tree-lined neighborhood in Overland Park, Kansas, a thirty-minute drive southeast of downtown Kansas City, just across the state line. The house had a large basement and an unfenced backyard. To my delight, I had my own television in my fully decorated bedroom, along with my own bathroom.

A block away was a new elementary school, to which I transferred soon after starting first grade. There were only three houses on our new street, which ended in a circular green. Here I learned to ride a bicycle and finally found some children my own age to play with.

Mom had made a few friends among the front-office wives and my schoolmates' mothers while we were living in the city, but she was lonely when we moved to the suburbs. Looking back, it all seems like an episode of the TV show *Mad Men*—couples doing everything that society said would make them happy, like having a child and moving to the suburbs as soon as they could, only to find out that it didn't make them happy at all.

LIVING WITH A HOUSEHOLD NAME

The name Finley didn't mean anything special in Dallas, where we lived in quiet anonymity. That changed when we moved to Kansas City. The word about our connection to the Athletics spread quickly through our new neighborhood, and in the spring teenage boys began to appear outside our house. They weren't there for me; I was just five years old. Those boys were there hoping to be seen by my Dad. They would stand outside our house and play catch, tossing a baseball back and forth, hoping Dad would "discover" them.

Sometimes they would greet Dad or Mom outside, saying, "Mr. Finley, my mom wanted me to show you how I pitch," or, "Mrs. Finley, would your husband consider letting me show him how I can throw?" This went on for months until, one day, two boys of thirteen were playing catch in the field next to our house. Perhaps they thought that if I participated, Dad would pay attention, so they asked me to stay in the field with them until Dad got home. I watched for a while, and then a baseball hit me in the chest. It hurt terribly. The boys ran over and apologized. I never told Mom, but somehow she and Dad found out, and no teenage boys came near our house again. Dad was easygoing and warm, but when he didn't like something, he put an end to it right away, especially if it involved his only child.

At school, kids started asking me how it felt to be a Finley. Because Charlie was rich, they assumed that Mom and Dad were wealthy, too. They weren't. "I'll bet you have everything you want," one classmate said to me. Or the boys would ask, "Have you met the ballplayers?" Sometimes I felt scrutinized by the parents of these children. The increasing questions, as well-meaning as they might have been, made me feel different, as if I wasn't part of the normal pack of kids. For a little girl in a new city, it wasn't a good feeling.

An incident in the second grade taught me that celebrity is a two-edged sword. For a history project, my teacher assigned each of us a classmate as a "partner." My partner and I worked on our project for several days and decided to sing a song. But the day before our presentation, my partner suddenly threatened me. She said if I did not bring her a popular Kansas City Athletics sticker for her notebook, then she would make me do our presentation alone.

It was my worst nightmare. Here I was, a six-year-old desperately trying to fit in at a new school among classmates who already viewed me as different because of my famous uncle. I often went out of my way to not make waves, and I rarely stood up for myself with my peers. But for some reason I decided this was the time to dig in my heels. I stood alone in front of the class and nervously sang *On Top of Old Smokey*. Somehow I got through my first experience with extortion.

Still yearning for acceptance from my peers, I began to use my baseball connections to attract friends. Uncle Charlie was the king of promotions, and Dad often came home with boxes of what was given out that day—caps, baseballs, and those coveted stickers. One evening, Dad brought home a box of kelly green Athletics baseball hats. I ran out to the front yard and gave these caps away to the kids in my neighborhood.

This year Charlie lost his beloved aunt Rose Marie, my grandmother. She was a kind and gracious woman, and Charlie adored her. Her death set him back for several months.

CHAPTER 9

BREAKING BARRIERS AND BEATLE MANIA

1963-1964-1965

E ach spring, Charlie would summon George Toma, the Kansas City Municipal Stadium groundskeeper, to his office. Charlie would make some small talk about the condition of the field, which was always impeccable. A diminutive man, in contrast to the elite athletes who played baseball or football on his well-maintained field, Toma was nevertheless a giant in his profession. He would soon become known as the best groundskeeper in the nation, and in the 1970s, the National Football League made him the official groundskeeper of the Super Bowl. But even in 1965, he was respected in the Athletics organization and throughout Kansas City.

Charlie liked him, too, and if anyone besides Carl Finley had job security with the Athletics, it was George Toma. So he was relaxed when he was told to report to the team owner. Toma found Charlie at his desk in an uncharacteristically quiet mood, almost humble.

Toma took a seat, and after a bit of chatting Charlie asked Toma about the teenagers on his staff, the part-time employees who worked on the grass and around the stadium. He then wrote a check for hundreds of dollars to pay for suits and ties for them so they would look sharp on their graduation day in June. Charlie, who was born in rural Alabama and worked in a steel mill as a teen, wanted to give the teenagers something he didn't have as a youth. It was the kind of generosity for which he rarely got credit. But Toma remembers.

"Charlie always took care of those kids," he recalled more than forty years later. "People like to say things about him, but I remember Charlie writing those checks and making sure those kids had what they needed."

Few Athletics fans were allowed to see that side of Charlie. One of the few in town who knew the truth was a lifelong Kansas Citian named Sam Gould. He owned the parking lot at Municipal Stadium when Charlie acquired the team in 1960. When Charlie infamously set the old "Yankees shuttle bus" on fire, it was parked temporarily in one of Gould's parking spaces.

Gould got along well with Dad and Charlie. "It was easy to work with Carl," he said. "He was a gentleman. A good man." Charlie, on the other hand, was more complex but still fair. One day, Gould received a phone call from Charlie, who thought that the fifty-cent parking fee might be preventing some fans from coming to games. He wanted to cut the price in half. Gould talked him out of it, persuading him that a price that low would hurt the team and put his parking company out of business. But Gould never forgot that conversation—it was the only time he could recall a sports owner asking to lower prices on *anything* for the fans.

Knowing that no ball club could survive on ticket sales to baseball purists alone, Charlie wanted to attract the casual fan and build baseball's popularity among a wider population. He still went in for novel promotions, especially if they involved bright colors. The team kept the controversial green, gold, and white uniforms introduced in 1963, but for 1964 they added two new shades: "sea foam green" and "wedding gown white." Charlie installed horns and flashing green and gold lights in Municipal Stadium, which went off whenever an Athletics player smacked a home run. And he officially changed the name of the team from the "Athletics" to the "A's." He wanted the name to sound more contemporary, and he thought "A's" was easier to say and write.

THE BEATLES

In February 1964, the Beatles made their famous American debut on the *Ed Sullivan Show*. Charlie got swept up in the ensuing Beatlemania and wanted to bring it to Kansas City. John, Paul, George, and Ringo performed all over the United States that summer, but Kansas City was not on their tour. Charlie decided to change that. Their usual performance fee was twenty-five thousand dollars, but the Liverpool lads demanded $150,000 to add Municipal Stadium to their tour on September 17, one of their few open days. Charlie announced that if he turned a profit from the concert, then he would donate a hundred thousand dollars to Children's Memorial Hospital in Kansas City.

Charlie was criticized then and now for his promotions, but he really believed that the future of professional sports depended on this kind of big entertainment event. His signature was printed on the tickets to the Beatles concert with the tagline "Today's Beatles fan is tomorrow's baseball fan." Charlie did his best to promote the concert.

A few weeks before the concert, Charlie persuaded Angels outfielder Jimmy Piersall to walk up to home plate wearing a Beatles mop-top wig for an at-bat, and Charlie himself was photographed in one. Dad and the rest of the front office were excited. As young as I was (six years old), I could sense my parents' anticipation. The day of the concert I came down with the measles, but it was such a big event that my mom took me anyway. I was quarantined in a team office with an open window facing the stage, partly because of my health and partly because of Dad's concern about the frenzied stadium crowd. Dad and Charlie hobnobbed with the band and their manager, Brian Epstein, in the team's executive office while girls outside screamed for the Fab Four before the concert. Dad commented that John, Paul, George, and Ringo were a "polite group of young men."

The Beatles sent the hometown crowd into a tizzy by kicking off the show with a Little Richard medley, "Kansas City/Hey, Hey, Hey, Hey"—a tip of the hat by the world's biggest pop stars to a legendary breeding ground of jazz and blues musicians. That had to have felt good to Kansas Citians. It made Dad happy. The Beatles played twelve songs in the thirty-one-minute concert. Dad's concerns about security proved well-founded when frenzied fans swarmed the stage, stopping the show.

None of this excitement apparently mattered to Mehl and the *Star*. Carrying its grudge against Charlie to new extremes, the paper refused to promote the concert and even refused to take Charlie's money for a paid advertisement, even though a well-attended performance would be a pop-culture coup for a city yearning for national respect, as well as guaranteeing Charlie's hundred-thousand-dollar donation to a hospital serving kids. Mehl blamed Charlie for the empty seats in Municipal Stadium that night, though the crowd of 20,280 was the second-largest in the Beatles' tour. Charlie himself was disappointed by the turnout (and remembered the experience when it was time to renegotiate the lease on Muni Stadium a few years later). He did not turn a profit but still donated twenty-five thousand dollars to the children's hospital.

The Beatles concert was yet another example of how Charlie and Dad were ahead of their time. So much of what they did was about growing the sport and trying to appeal to kids and the casual fan. Today, sports franchises pay consultants enormous fees to expand their markets and increase TV ratings and ticket and merchandise sales, but Charlie and Dad came up with these ideas themselves.

BETTY CAYWOOD

On September 18, 1964, the Athletics were in New York to play the Yankees. The worst team in baseball was playing the best, and the game looked like it. The Yanks blanked the Athletics 6–0 in front of 16,094 fans in the Bronx. But regardless of what happened on the field that day, the Athletics made history up in the announcer's booth when Betty Caywood made her debut with the Athletics' play-by-play team. Charlie had hired the thirty-two-year-old TV weather analyst from Chicago, making her the first woman to broadcast a Major League Baseball game. It was no accident that her debut was in New York City, as Charlie wanted the maximum exposure in the nation's biggest market for the pioneering event.

For the final fifteen games of the '64 season, Caywood provided color commentary while Monte Moore and Bill Bryson did the play-by-play. An attractive young blonde, Caywood was bound to appeal to Charlie, and she was actually a pretty good announcer. She had received her master's degree in speech from Northwestern University. When Charlie met her in Chicago, he learned that they shared a baseball connection with Athletics past and present—Betty knew Connie Mack III and had befriended the *Kansas City Star*'s sportswriter Joe McGuff and his wife, Kay. In a moment of inspiration, Charlie offered Betty a job. She accepted.

Still, Charlie was an enigma to her, as he was to so many others. In general he treated her well, she said. He covered her moving costs from Chicago to Kansas City and the costs of her childcare. But he did one thing Betty really didn't like—he tried to tell her what to wear during her broadcasts. Specifically, he wanted her in a gold-colored blouse and a green skirt. "I replied, 'When you have your male broadcasters wear green and yellow, I'll be happy to do so, too," Betty recalls. Like Dad and other A's staff, Betty was the recipient of Charlie's middle-of-the-night telephone calls. She handled them by hanging up.

It turned out that a broadcasting career did not appeal to Betty, and she quit when the season ended on October 3 with—what else?—a loss. "I love baseball today because of that short period in my life," she says. "But for all the money [Charlie] spent on me, why, it was ridiculous."

PICKING UP THE PACE WITH THE PITCHOMETER

Charlie understood that the American attention span was getting shorter and shorter and that it led to complaints about the slow pace of baseball games. If baseball was to survive the competition against constant-action sports like football, hockey, and basketball, it would have to pick up its pace. Taking a cue from Bill Veeck's Comiskey Park, Charlie installed a "Pitchometer" on the scoreboard to time pitchers. A rarely enforced MLB rule gave the pitcher only twenty seconds after receiving the ball from the catcher to make his throw if no one was on base. Veeck's Pitchometer had been disallowed as soon as it was put up in 1960, and the device was never used in a Major League game.

That is, not until the 1965 season, when Charlie tried it. The Pitchometer on the Municipal Stadium scoreboard was actually used for a few weeks in April, the announcer urging fans to monitor it, before league officials squashed it. Once again, MLB's old boys club didn't appreciate Charlie's innovations, and they went out of their way to try to put him in his place. The obscure twenty-second rule was enforced for the first time in anyone's memory against the Athletics' Diego Segui—twice—the umpire adding a ball to the count each time. The Pitchometer had already been taken down, but league officials were determined to punish Charlie for even trying the innovation.

A NEW MASCOT

Charlie and Dad appreciated the power of animals to capture the public's attention. Charlie decided it was time to replace the team's elephant mascot, which he had inherited from the previous owners.

Toward the end of the 1964 season, Charlie, Aunt Shirley, Dad, Mom, and all of us young cousins gathered at the Muehlebach after a game to discuss the possibilities. Charlie suggested a skunk. Dad smiled and chuckled. "Well," he said, "it would get us a lot of attention."

"Yes!" exclaimed Charlie.

"You know the other team will trot from the dugout holding their noses. And just imagine the headlines when we lose a game; 'A's Skunked Again!'"

Charlie look a bit crestfallen. The skunk idea was never mentioned again.

One thing we all agreed on—we did not want the elephant. The previous owner had gone with an elephant, and we wanted to distance the franchise from the old regime. And elephants are fat, clumsy, and slow—not the image we wanted for our A's.

Nothing final was decided, but it triggered my imagination. At home, in my bedroom, I began drawing different animals—some clad in green and gold, some not—to see how they might look. We went into the off-season after the '64 campaign still in search of a mascot. Then, a few weeks before the '65 season opening, Governor Warren Hearnes made the choice for us. He gave Charlie a Missouri mule.

THE MOST FAMOUS MULE IN THE WORLD

A symbol of stubbornness, mules are popular in the Show Me State. Charlie was delighted with the creature and immediately realized he had found his mascot. Sportswriters and the other owners, as usual, found something to complain about. But even the most cynical players were amused by it, and the fans loved the mule. Nearly fifty years later, it still is one of the first things that people associate with the Athletics' Finley years.

Charlie named the mule after himself—Charlie O. "I thought we should name this mule after an ass," he'd bellow with a big laugh. His jokes never stopped. "Do you want to be my friend? First, kiss my ass." One day Charlie's friend Ed Daly, the former president of World Airways, jumped on the mule before the start of a game and rode around the field. Watching the game on TV in Chicago, Charlie called the dugout and had them take a message to Daly. "Hey! Get off my ass, will ya?"

Having finally found his mascot, Charlie went into overdrive with his promotional ideas. He got the mule an air-conditioned trailer equipped with a phonograph to play songs like "The Mule Train." He had a baseball hat made for the animal, complete with ear holes, and gave it a green and gold blanket imprinted with "Charlie O." Charlie built a special stable in the petting zoo behind the left-field wall, next to the picnic area, and the mule moved in with the monkeys, sheep, rabbits, and pheasants.

On Opening Day Governor Hearnes officially presented the mule to Charlie, who donned a cowboy hat and rode his new namesake around the ballpark. Charlie O's duties would not be confined to Municipal Stadium. He went on the road to every American League city, spending the night in a trailer behind the players' hotel. Before games, Charlie would ride his mule through the city streets, sometimes ending up in the hotel lobby, to the chagrin of hotel employees and the shock of local sportswriters.

When the Athletics were in New York City to play the Yankees, for example, Charlie proudly rode his Missouri mount through Times Square, then to a barbershop for a shave, and into his hotel lobby, where Charlie O demonstrated that he was not housebroken. Wherever Charlie O showed up, people were charmed. Women, in particular, found him irresistibly cute. He created a sensation everywhere he went.

The only place Charlie O was not welcome was Chicago, where the White Sox' co-owner, Arthur Allyn, refused to admit the mule to Comiskey Park. Uncle Charlie responded in the way most people did in the 1960s when they felt wronged—he staged a protest. He held a luncheon at the Sheraton-Chicago Hotel for Charlie O and hired attractive young women to picket Comiskey Park. Meanwhile, a squad of police officers had been dispatched to the ballpark for the sole purpose of keeping the mule out. While the policemen kept their eyes fixed on Charlie O, the A's sneaked a baby mule into the back of the park, and outfielder Ken Harrelson triumphantly rode it onto the field in the middle of the game. The umpires called time and kicked the mule—and Harrelson—off the field. Meanwhile, Uncle Charlie—having exacted his revenge—pointed to Allyn and laughed.

Back in Kansas City, some of the older denizens of the petting zoo suffered unhappier fates (this is long before society took an enlightened approach to animal welfare). One sheep died after a home-run ball landed on its head, while another passed away from a heart attack while being chased around the zoo by an Athletics player. The pitcher Moe Drabowsky would use a fungo bat to hit the animals with a baseball before games, while young hurlers Catfish Hunter and Lew Krausse found a way to drug the monkeys. They would capture grasshoppers in the outfield, stuff sleeping pills in the grasshoppers' throats, and then feed them to the monkeys. Catfish and Krausse would howl with laughter when the animals jumped around the cages while under the influence. Something like that today would get players suspended and fined, of course.

But Charlie O never received that kind of abuse. In fact, it became a pregame tradition of sorts for a player to ride the mule onto the field near the grandstand so fans could pet it as it made the rounds. Charlie O would then take a bow and be led away.

Charlie O once found himself in a fist-fight with the player who was leading him around the field for the fans. The animal stepped on the player's foot. The player let out a yelp and punched Charlie O on the shoulder. The mule, with eyes bulging, jumped back before the player could release his hold on the lead rope, leaving him flat on the ground. Then Charlie O began to walk slowly but directly at him. Everyone familiar with the mule knew he didn't have a mean bone in his body. He was simply perplexed to see a man in that odd position. When he approached the fallen player, the man jumped up and ran a few steps away, brushing off his derriere and giving an angry look at Charlie O. The scene caused a stir in the stands, some spectators laughing and some shouting advice. Eventually he picked up the rope again and led Charlie O off the field.

Dad and Charlie eventually decided to keep the mule at Benjamin Stables, owned and managed by Howard Benjamin, with whom Dad had a warm friendship. Howard gave me my own pony, Tom Thumb, a black horse with white markings and just the right size for a seven-year-old. Riding Tom gave me my love of horses and all things Western. When Mom took me to Benjamin Stables to ride my pony, I would visit Charlie O too and feed him sugar cubes or carrots that I smuggled in.

CHARLIE'S FAST CROWD

One evening in April 1965, while the two families were dining out together, we ran into a woman whom my parents and the Benjamins knew. A striking sometime model in her late twenties, she had a sultry air that made it hard not to look at her. She was part of the fun-loving baseball crowd that Charlie led, a group Mom grew to loathe—with good reason, it would turn out.

CHAPTER 10

SEEDS OF SUCCESS

MID-1960S

Three years after Charlie acquired the Athletics—and despite Ernie Mehl's efforts—he began to receive credit for some of the changes he had made.

The readers of Bob Mussman's sports column in the *Chillicothe Tribune* lived a hundred miles northeast from Kansas City, but in 1963 he urged them to go take in an A's game: "The beautiful stadium alone is worth the trip. It combines a muted shade of green, coral orange and cream in the seating area. The well-tended field, the envy of any ardent lawnman, is surrounded by red shale track." But the stadium wasn't the only attraction. Mussman noted that "under controversial Charles Finley, the A's have been making strides toward the goal of building a winning ball club." He continued, "The A's have given up their policy of trades with the Yankees, and now are doing some effective building through a well managed farm team." He credited the organization with "what appears to be an expert managerial and coaching staff" and declared that "this is no longer a team of losers."

Despite Charlie's spending and his never-ending promotions, the Kansas City Athletics in the mid-1960s were still a joke in baseball circles—on the field, in the standings, and at the box office. Charlie and Dad, proud and competitive men, desperately wanted to change that. They knew that the best and cheapest way to build a winner was through the franchise's farm system. That idea wasn't revolutionary. Finding and developing young talent and then letting it mature in the minor leagues was a time-honored strategy. But if it were easy, then every franchise's farm system would be brimming with talent. Few actually were. Executing that plan took good scouts, a smart general manager and player personnel executive, a little luck, and—perhaps most importantly—a generous owner.

If you asked any team owner or manager, he would say, sure, his farm teams were important. But everyone seemed to treat the farm teams as an afterthought. Charlie's main focus was finding and signing up prospects, and after years of quietly going about "watering the plants," his farm team was perhaps his best-kept secret. He did not look for quick and easy ways to build a competitive team. "I have to think about the next ten years," he said.

Charlie elaborated in an interview in 1968: "I decided a long time ago that we'd have to start raising our own ballplayers. It's the only way. It's like building a house; you have to have a solid foundation no matter how much it costs. I think we have it now." Looking back in 1996, Marvin Miller, the head of the baseball players union, agreed: "He was his own scouting system. He personally recruited the bulk of that team. I knew nobody in baseball who could ever approach what he did."

Charlie started acquiring young talent as soon as he took over. He signed the pitcher Lew Krausse Jr. in 1961 for $150,000, then a pro baseball record. His scouts signed the Cuban-born Dagoberto "Bert" Campaneris for just a few thousand dollars in 1962. A year later, Charlie grabbed Dave Duncan as an amateur free agent straight out of high school, when the feisty catcher was just a skinny teenager. That same season, Charlie signed the pitcher Paul Lindblad, an underrated reliever who would play for the Athletics organization until 1976 (save for a year and half with other teams in 1971–1972). In 1964, the big catch was Jim Hunter, a North Carolina farm boy whose brother had shot off his toe in a hunting accident. Charlie sent him to the Mayo Clinic for treatment, and Hunter convalesced at his farm in LaPorte, Indiana. Charlie gave him the nickname "Catfish" when he began pitching for the A's in 1965.

Charlie isn't remembered for spending a lot of money on players, but he certainly went all-out to land young talent in the 1960s. 1964 was the year that Charlie and his scouting staff really got on a roll. By the time they were done, they had assembled one of the most outstanding pools of young talent in baseball history—playmakers who, a decade later, were the heart of the only non-Yankees dynasty in baseball's modern era.

Charlie kicked off the year by wooing John Odom, an amateur free agent from Macon, Georgia. Demonstrating the team's emphasis on youth, Charlie personally made the trip down south to Odom's home on the night of his high school graduation. Growing up in Alabama had taught Charlie something about Southern hospitality, and he showed up with groceries and cooked dinner for Odom's family. He charmed them with a dinner menu of corn bread, fried chicken, corn on the cob, black-eyed peas, and collard greens. Nicknamed "Blue Moon" because he rarely smiled and often seemed sad, Odom wasn't glum after Charlie's visit. The kid signed for a seventy-five-thousand-dollar bonus in June 1964. "I'd have signed for as little as thirty-five thousand," Odom told reporters years later.

Next, Charlie signed hometown talent Chuck Dobson, who grew up just an outfielder's throw away from Municipal Stadium in Kansas City. Dobson signed for twenty-five thousand dollars in 1964. Rollie Fingers was signed as an amateur free agent in 1964 at the tender age of eighteen with a signing bonus of twenty thousand dollars. Nearly thirty years later, he would be inducted into the Hall of Fame. Next was Joe Rudi, a lanky California kid also signed to an amateur free agent contract after going undrafted.

Charlie was just getting started. He drafted Rick Monday in the first round of the 1965 MLB draft and then signed the highly touted prospect to a $104,000 bonus. That same day, he drafted a twenty-one-year-old third baseman named Salvatore Bando and agreed to a sixty-five-thousand-dollar bonus. The following year, 1966, Charlie drafted a young outfielder named Reginald Martinez Jackson, paying the Arizona State University star better known as "Reggie" a ninety-five-thousand-dollar bonus. In 1967, Charlie made his way down to Mansfield, Louisiana, to sign the Athletics' second-round pick, a young hurler and college football star named Vida Blue. Charlie paid the nineteen-year-old a signing bonus of forty thousand dollars.

And that isn't even counting players like Claude "Skip" Lockwood and Jumbo Jim Nash, pitchers signed by the Athletics in the mid-1960s who went on to have productive major league careers, albeit mostly with other teams. Second baseman Dick Green was the only Athletics player to be part of the 1970s dynasty who was signed with the squad before Uncle Charlie bought the franchise in late 1960. Yet he spent his entire major league career with the organization—1963 to 1974—under Charlie's watch.

Nearly all of these young stars would be important members of the championship teams of the early '70s. But back then, they were all skinny, wide-eyed kids with oodles of raw talent but little polish. Charlie was the owner behind those signing bonuses, which totaled several hundreds of thousands of dollars when the dust cleared. Not bad for a team owner known for being "too cheap."

THE SOUL OF THE WINNER

Charlie didn't just sign the checks. More importantly, he was making the final decisions to take these guys. The *Oakland Tribune* beat writer Ron Bergman once said that Charlie "could look into a man's soul and tell if he were a winner or not." That may sound strange or even laughable to today's numbers-crazy fans and reporters—and to the growing number of experts who value statistics and cold numbers over their own perceptions and intuition. But it was true. Charlie's intuition would pay off a few years later, before baseball teams were relying on computers. Charlie could judge people and their intangibles better than anyone. And as Bergman pointed out, it's hard to argue with the results, especially once he got involved with player personnel decisions.

Charlie became known as a hands-on owner—what the sports media like to call a "meddler." Though other people often held the title of general manager—including Frank Lane, Pat Friday, and Hank Peters—in reality, Charlie was the team's real general manager, and Dad was his partner. Few player personnel decisions were made without Charlie's and Dad's consent or outright participation.

When the A's started winning, the jealous MLB owners concocted a revisionist history that minimized Charlie's contribution to the team's success. If Charlie's role was to be diminished, then someone had to be credited for building this championship team. The man they came up with for that role was Hank Peters, who worked in the front office in the early and mid-1960s. Peters had a great career as a baseball executive, building winning teams in Baltimore in the 1970s and Cleveland in the late 1980s before retiring in 1992. But Peters left the A's after the 1966 season, and he wasn't around for major acquisitions like Vida Blue, the hiring of Dick Williams as team manager, or the excellent, one-sided trades that Charlie made for Ken Holtzman or Billy North or Ray Fosse. Those deals took the Athletics from mere contenders to world champions, and Charlie was the driving force behind all of them.

Nevertheless, one part of the revisionist history is correct. Charlie had someone helping him and giving him advice on players. That man was Carl Finley.

ROBBED

To this day, Kansas City fans feel like they were robbed. They cheered those young players Reggie Jackson, Vida Blue, Catfish Hunter, Sal Bando, and many others when they were still green, only to see the glory and World Series titles go to another city after Charlie moved the franchise to Oakland. Accurately or not, that's how many a forlorn Midwestern Athletics fan still sees it. Given how Dad's contributions were overlooked, and still are today, I think he could relate to how those Kansas City baseball fans felt.

CHAPTER 11

THE ROAD TO FREEDOM

1966

A fter we moved to suburban Overland Park, Dad started to spend more time at his office at Municipal Stadium, a half-hour drive from our house, and Mom grew suspicious. I suppose her doubts began when Dad brought home that autographed photo of Connie Stevens a few years earlier, and her suspicions only deepened when she saw the glamorous crowd, with plenty of young, attractive women, at Charlie's post-game parties at the Muehlebach Hotel.

Eventually, Mom discovered that her suspicions were justified. One rainy, wind-blown night, she found Dad's new Ford Thunderbird in the parking lot of the Conga Room, a dive on the outskirts of town. She went inside and spotted Dad, wearing a cowboy hat, with the sultry young woman we'd met several months earlier in the restaurant with the Benjamins. Mom and Dad separated in January 1966, and Dad moved back into the Muehlebach Hotel. The next month Mom filed for divorce, citing "gross neglect and extreme cruelty."

The world Charlie inhabited, and into which he had drawn my father, was hard on marriages. Word around the franchise was that this same young woman had also had affairs with Charlie and Howard Benjamin. The Benjamins' marriage and Charlie's fell apart in due course.

Mom and I moved back to Dallas in July 1966, a few months before I started the third grade. We lived in a modest but comfortable duplex about three blocks away from my new school. Dad, who stayed in Kansas City, paid the rent for the first six months. No longer a housewife, Mom took a job as a first-grade teacher at another school in town.

THE PLAYERS' ASSOCIATION

The Athletics finished the 1966 season 74–86—not great, but much better than in years past, and the squad seemed ready to escape its longtime laughingstock status. Charlie was halfway through his four-year lease extension at Municipal Stadium. As attendance dwindled and his relationship with Kansas City's leaders and fans deteriorated, it became clear that a move lay ahead. Charlie eyed other cities for the team—Louisville, Oakland, and especially Dallas—any place, really, where he could escape his own unhappy "marriage" with the Midwest.

But in baseball that year, there was an even more important development, one that would change the game irrevocably. The players—who were seeking freedom themselves—recruited a respected national labor official to lead their union, called the Major League Baseball Players' Association.

The Players' Association had been around for years, but it had never been effective. The players weren't unified, and they lacked a leader with the guts and expertise to lead a truly solid labor organization. Before the mid-1960s, any players' group had been a "company union"—more window dressing than a real union representing players' interests—and it never challenged the owners of MLB's twenty franchises. But the players' anger and resentment toward the owners had been festering for years, even decades. The average player's salary in 1966 was just nineteen thousand dollars per year. The minimum annual salary was six thousand dollars. (Today, the average player gets $2.7 million per year, and the minimum is $380,000.) What really angered the players was the Reserve Clause, which tied players for life to the baseball franchise they had signed with as a youngster. A player could move to another team only if he was cut or traded by management. If he wanted more money, the only thing he could do was hold out—that is, refuse to show up to play until he got a raise—something only a few stars ever tried. There was no such thing as a "free agent" in 1966, and there wouldn't be for almost a decade.

The MLB Players' Association's new executive director was a tough, smart, and respected negotiator with years of experience negotiating labor contracts for the United Steelworkers and the United Auto Workers. His name was Marvin Miller. In 1992, Hall of Fame broadcaster Red Barber called him "one of the two or three most important men in baseball history."

When Miller took over the MLBPA, his first mission was to educate all of the ballplayers on their rights and the goals of their organization. Miller was the pick of the activist players, but there were plenty of others who, fearful of losing their jobs, were quick to believe the smear campaign that baseball's commissioner and top officials had started against him. Indeed, Miller found that baseball's brass was telling some players behind the scenes that he could not be trusted and, even worse, that he was a communist.

Miller always rebutted such talk by saying he wanted the players to make more money for themselves, which required that the franchises turn a healthy profit. What was more capitalist than that? Miller spent the first couple of years laying the groundwork and building trust between the union and the players.

The battles that Miller would fight against the commissioner and the owners, including Uncle Charlie, were still years away. To the casual fan, the business of baseball looked the same as it had for almost seventy years. But changes were brewing. Skirmishes between players and owners had popped up through the years (a young Joe DiMaggio had held out for more money from the Yankees in the late 1930s), but there had been nothing like the rancor that was about to break out. Major League Baseball would have as bumpy a ride through the second half of the 1960s as the rest of America.

CHAPTER 12

TAKE THAT GUN TO THE TRAIN STATION

1966-1967

Among other odd things, 1967 was the year one of the team members, Campy Campaneris, was sued for paternity. That may not have been unusual among professional sportsmen, but Charlie was named as a co-defendant in the suit. The plaintiff sought four hundred thousand dollars in damages from Charlie, alleging that he knew of the paternity claim and helped Campy elude process servers whenever the team played in Anaheim, California.

Amid the theatrics that seemed to accompany Charlie and his team on and off the field, a quiet change had taken place. It wasn't so much what had happened as what *hadn't* happened. The annual pillaging of the Athletics had ended—the best talent hadn't been traded off to the Yankees! Suddenly, the A's were everyone's pick to contend for the pennant in 1967. *Sports Illustrated* put their manager, Alvin Dark, on its March 12 cover with the caption "Dark's Outlook is Young and Bright." Kansas City fans had hope for the future for the first time since the team arrived in 1955.

GUNSHOTS IN THE NIGHT

Lew Krausse Jr. had been pitching in the major leagues off and on since Charlie signed him out of high school in 1961. He was still boyish-looking—lanky, blond, and freckle-faced—but on this squad full of greenhorns, he had become the "old man" on the roster.

He stood out in other ways, too. By his own admission, he drank too much. But that wasn't anything new in baseball. What made him different was that he could be eccentric, bombastic, and flakey, long before sports fans and the media appreciated those traits. He also stood up to Charlie whenever it suited him. And Charlie appreciated that. He respected people who stood up for themselves, even when he was the guy they were standing up against.

A lot of the players lived in the Bellerive Hotel, a luxury apartment hotel built in 1922 in Kansas City's Hyde Park neighborhood, not far from my parents' Janssen Place home. Krausse, who lived on the top floor, said it was an open secret that Charlie paid the hotel manager to spy on players. Despite his suspicion that the team owner was watching, Krausse wasn't afraid to have a good time, and he had already earned a reputation as a free spirit. He even started a late-night routine that would have fit right in with Kansas City's Wild West days a century before. Just about every night, Krausse came home drunk, and before going to sleep he fired a pistol out his window into the air. "My uncle, a game warden in Pennsylvania, once gave me a .38 revolver," Krausse explained. "A lot of the players, we were living in rooms way up high in this hotel, so it became part of my deal, my nightly routine. When I came home, I'd fire a gun out the window and then go to bed."

Remarkably, this went on for months until the hotel hosted a convention in June 1967 and moved the players down to the second floor. Krausse had pitched the first game of a doubleheader against the Detroit Tigers at Municipal Stadium. He was shelled, chased early from the game, and the A's lost eleven to one. The pitcher stopped off at a bar to drink off his frustration and became intoxicated as usual. "I came home that night and opened the window and fired the gun in the air twice," he said. "Obviously, it was goofy, but it was my trademark." His nightly routine completed, Krausse shut the window and went to sleep. Just like every other "normal" night. The next morning however, was anything but normal.

At 6 a.m. the phone rang in the hotel room. Krausse, tired and hung over, picked up the phone. It was Charlie, and he got to the point quickly. "Do you have a gun?"

Krausse always gave it to him straight. "Yes."

Charlie replied, "You take that gun to the train station and put it in a box."

Still shaking off the cobwebs, Krausse suddenly got really scared. "Wait, what? Why? What happened?"

Charlie repeated himself, but more urgently, "Just take it to a train station and put it in a box."

He did exactly what Charlie told him. He took a cab to the train station, rented a locker, and hid the pistol there. The trench coat he wore to hide the .38 must have made him conspicuous in the Kansas City summer heat. Nervous as hell, the ballplayer knew there was a Phillips Petroleum building across the street from the hotel. He had a sick feeling that he had killed somebody with an errant gunshot.

Krauss returned to the hotel and went to his room, intending to call Charlie. But that proved to be difficult. "I got to my room and there were ten people in there—cops and people from Phillips Petroleum, mostly," Krausse recalled. "They were dusting the windowsill and I was just waiting to get handcuffed."

Krausse took Charlie's advice and said nothing. He learned that striking employees were picketing outside the Phillips building. The company and the police wanted to know if a union picketer had fired the gunshot. When they found that the culprit was a half-crazy pitcher from the home team, the authorities lost interest in the case, especially with Charlie smooth-talking the police and making it clear he supported Krausse. "They didn't want to press charges," Krausse said. "It was all over and done with."

Most sports owners would have been furious and would have cracked down on the ballplayers. Not Charlie. He saw it as an adventure, a game of hide-and-seek of sorts, something that spoke to the adolescent prankster in him. It helped that he was personally fond of Krausse, his first baseball bonus baby. But, there was something about outwitting authority figures that always fueled Charlie. So, instead of seeing the gun incident as a professional headache, Charlie saw it as a chance for fun and games.

"I called Charlie and told him what happened, that all those cops were there. He just started laughing," Krausse said. "He told me some story that there was a cleaning lady in the Phillips building. He exaggerated and told me the bullet was ricocheting around the room and the cleaning lady had to hit the deck. He made a big joke of the whole thing."

In fact, a woman staying next door to Krausse had reported the gunshot to the front desk clerk, who called the hotel manager. The hotel manager then called Charlie, who then called Krausse.

"I still have the gun," says Krausse. "I don't fire it anymore—well, maybe on New Year's Eve, but most of the time I can't stay up until midnight on New Year's anymore."

WHAT HAPPENED ON FLIGHT 85?

On August 3, the A's lost an extra-inning game to the Red Sox in Boston, and the next day they hopped on TWA Flight 85 for Kansas City. Stops in Baltimore and St. Louis turned what was normally a two-and-a-half-hour flight into a six-hour ordeal instead.

There weren't many people on the weekday flight, so the stewardesses passed around alcohol, and some of the players imbibed more than others. As the players told it, the flight was no different from dozens of flights a ball club makes each season—a few drinks, some laughs and off-color stories, maybe a little flirting with the stewardesses, then landing on the tarmac and off to the hotel, whether on the road or back at the Bellerive in Kansas City. But I overheard Dad tell a friend that some players had apparently gotten carried away, pinching and grabbing one of the stewardesses until she fled to the front of the plane and begged for protection.

Two weeks later, the A's were on another road trip, this time in Washington, D.C. The phone rang at 8 a.m. in Lew Krausse's room in the Shoreham Hotel. It was Charlie. He explained that he was fining Krausse five hundred dollars for drinking and using profanity on "that flight." Krausse wasn't sure what flight his boss was talking about. Once Charlie explained, Krausse started defending himself. "But I didn't do anything," he said. Within seconds they were screaming at each other, until Krausse slammed down the receiver.

A few minutes later, the phone rang again. "I'm suspending you immediately without pay for conduct unbecoming of a Major Leaguer," Charlie said.

"For what? I didn't do anything!" Krausse yelled again into the phone. This time, Charlie hung up on Krausse.

He wanted the team image to be wholesome, even if his own behavior crossed the line of propriety occasionally. Charlie had the following statement posted on the clubhouse bulletin board:

> Effective immediately and for the balance of the season, all alcoholic drinks will no longer be served on commercial airlines to members of the Kansas City Athletics.
>
> The Kansas City Athletics will no longer tolerate the shenanigans of a few individuals who obviously do not appreciate the privilege of playing in the major leagues and being treated like gentlemen.
>
> The attitude, actions and words of some of you have been deplorable. As a member of Organized Baseball, you have certain responsibilities and obligations to yourself, your family, your club and most important of all—the fans. To the vast majority of you who have always conducted yourselves as gentlemen on and off the playing field, I sincerely regret the necessity of this action.

When they saw the clubhouse letter, the A's players were upset. Some of them, led by Ken Harrelson and relief pitcher and union representative

Jack Aker, went to Alvin Dark's hotel room to complain. They told the manager that they were going to release a statement of their own. Dark said that was okay, but he wanted to see a draft of it first to make sure it didn't get them into deeper trouble. Aker and Harrelson agreed.

Meanwhile, Charlie and Dad had flown TWA to Washington and checked into the Shoreham Hotel to quell the trouble. They met with Dark and asked him to support ownership regarding Krausse's suspension. Dark refused. Charlie fired him on the spot, though the three men stayed in the room and kept discussing the ball club. After a few shots of J&B scotch and further conversation, Dark even predicted that the A's would win the American League pennant by 1971—less than four years away.

It was a typical Charlie episode—reacting swiftly and with some anger but not making it personal. Suddenly Charlie softened. He offered Dark a contract, even though Dad reminded him that he had just fired Dark. "How 'bout two more years? With a raise," Charlie said.

Deal. Charlie, Dad, and Dark celebrated by liberally sharing more J&B. It was a nice evening—until the *Kansas City Star* beat writer Paul O'Boynick knocked on Charlie's door and asked what Charlie thought about the players' statement. "What players' statement?" Charlie asked.

Uh-oh.

The players had released a statement, ignoring their manager's request to show it to him first. O'Boynick read the statement to Charlie:

> In response to Charles O. Finley's statement of August 18, we, the players of the Kansas City Athletics, feel that an unjust amount of pressure has been brought to bear on several members of the club who had no part whatsoever in the so-called incident on the recent plane trip from Boston to Kansas City. The overwhelming opinion of the players is that the entire matter was blown out of proportion. Mr. Finley's policy of using certain unauthorized personnel in his organization as go-betweens has led to similar misunderstandings in the past and has tended to undermine the morale of the club. We players feel

that if Mr. Finley would give his fine coaching staff and excellent manager the authority they deserve, these problems would not exist.

FIRED UP AND FIRED AGAIN

Charlie soon found out that Dark knew about the letter but had not told him about it. The next day, Charlie fired Dark again and replaced him with Luke Appling. That day's ballgame was rained out, and a reporter called Harrelson for his comments about his manager's firing. The next day, Harrelson was quoted in the Washington newspapers and on the television news as saying, "Charlie Finley is a menace to baseball."

Charlie called Harrelson the next morning, asking him if he really said that. "I said everything except you were a menace," Harrelson said. "What I actually said to the reporter was that I thought your actions of the last few days were bad for baseball."

Charlie asked him to publicly retract the statement. Harrelson replied that he would retract the "menace" part but he stood by everything else. Charlie called back about thirty minutes later to tell Harrelson he had released him from the A's. The team could have made fifty thousand dollars by trading the outfielder in a waiver wire deal, but Charlie refused, saying, "It would have been blood money."

The players, then and now, blamed the play-by-play announcer Monte Moore for "snitching" on them about their behavior on the airplane. When word got around that the players didn't trust Moore any longer, the announcer told Charlie that he was worried about traveling with them. Charlie assured the players Monte was not a spy, but the players never believed him. Many of the players still blame Moore, but I happen to know that Monte wasn't the spy on the plane.

Monte had flown numerous times with the players, and what happened on Flight 85 was nothing new. Besides, Monte was the type to "tune out" what was happening. But Charlie's eleven-year-old son Paul was on that plane, seated in the front row. He told Dad that he had heard some stewardesses in distress. They were trying to be nice, but the abuse became unbearable, and one of them ran to the front of the plane and sat near Paul. She said she felt safe there. The frightened boy's account of the flight to his father explains Charlie's uncharacteristically censorious reaction.

GLASSES TO THE WALL

Charlie didn't spend that *entire* trip to Washington playing the disciplinarian. One evening he and Dad noticed an attractive airline stewardess stroll down the hall in their hotel and knock on the door of the room next to theirs, which was occupied by a member of the team. The man answered the door and quietly ushered her in. Charlie and Dad hustled back into their room and, with the aid of a couple of empty drinking glasses held up to the wall, joined in the fun, as it were, as unseen and uninvited guests. Dad told me he worried that their amorous colleague would hear their stifled laughter and suppressed snorting through the wall, but nothing was said the next morning.

CHAPTER 13

DON'T CRY FOR ME, KANSAS CITY

1967

Bette Davis in *All about Eve* says as she goes up the stairs, "Fasten your seatbelts. It's going to be a bumpy night." She might have been talking to Charlie and Dad as they arrived for the June 1967 meeting of a lame-duck city council. The newly elected council would take office the next morning, but the councilmen whose terms were expiring called this emergency meeting on their last night in office hoping to finalize a lease agreement with the A's. Arriving half an hour early, the Finleys walked by the clerk's desk and picked up copies of the agenda then took seats in the front row. A kind of electric stress pervaded the chamber. Charlie and Dad spotted writers for the *Kansas City Star* toward the back.

The Athletics' 1964 lease of Municipal Stadium would expire on December 31, 1967, but Charlie and Dad were there to try one more time to get a reasonable renewal. The last rent check for twenty-five thousand dollars under the old lease would come due in August. By the middle of the 1967 season, there was little optimism about baseball in Kansas City.

The new council wanted a commitment from Charlie that the team would stay in town for at least four more years. Charlie wanted a fairer deal, one like the Kansas City Chiefs enjoyed, with only a two-year term.

As they disposed of the preliminary items on the agenda, the city councilmen's eyes flitted nervously between Charlie and Dad in the front row and the business at hand. At last the chairman announced the item everyone was waiting for—whether the city and the Kansas City Athletics could agree on a renewal of the lease.

Days of intense negotiating sessions with Charlie and Dad leading up to this meeting had left both the council and the Finleys optimistic about closing a deal, but it wasn't certain. The city manager gave a brief report and identified some areas of disagreement. The two hot items remaining to be settled were the amount of the rent and the escape clause, but there were two other big issues in the background—the question of a new stadium and the relentless animosity of local sports media—chiefly the *Kansas City Star*.

When the city manager finished his report, the chairman invited Charlie to address the council. The councilmen's faces betrayed their worry. They wanted to keep the franchise in Kansas City. If the A's moved out, it could be years before they got a new team. But there were lots of others in town who wanted Charlie gone. Charlie spoke in his typical deliberate manner, fixing his dark brown "talon-like" eyes (as Bowie Kuhn would call them) on his audience. His occasional smiles didn't seem to relax the apprehensive councilmen.

Throughout the negotiations on the renewal of the lease, the *Kansas City Star* sports writers had relentlessly criticized Charlie, trying to discredit him with rumors that, despite the huge sums he had spent on improvements to Municipal Stadium, he intended to move to Dallas, Louisville, Oakland, or some other city. Ernie Mehl in particular, now half-retired, continued his vendetta against Charlie, who could do nothing right. The effect of the constant bad press could be seen in the team's annual "Official Score Book." The 1965 edition carried display ads for TWA, the Hotel Muehlebach, the Shoreham, the Leamington, and Hamm's beer. By 1967 the ads for the major hotels had been replaced by ads for "Cat Balleu—featuring Strip-O-Rama," Lorillard Cigarettes, and Quick & Easy Loans.

Charlie brought up his key issues. Under the 1964 lease, the A's were paying fifty thousand dollars a year, but the city now wanted five hundred thousand dollars a year. Charlie was willing to compromise. He knew that for political reasons the council was unlikely to renew the 1964 terms, and he offered $250,000 a year for rent. Even that number would be a strain on franchise cash-flow. Dad, who handled the books and the ticket sales, paid the bills, signed off on the lineup for each game, handled public relations, and owned a minority share of the franchise, squirmed imperceptibly when Charlie uttered the figure.

Charlie then proposed virtually the same escape clause that was in the 1963 lease and from which former owner Arnold Johnson had benefited. If attendance dropped below a certain figure, Charlie would be released from the lease and free to move the franchise out of town. Attendance had been poor since 1963. A council member spoke up, objecting that attendance was virtually certain to come in under the figure in the escape clause. But Charlie optimistically suggested that attendance could be improved with the city's help. Several of the council members cautiously nodded their heads.

As Charlie spoke, an exaggerated cough could occasionally be heard. Dad looked over his shoulder and saw Ernie Mehl, who smirked at him. Always the gentlemen, Dad replied with a slightly sardonic smile.

When he concluded, Charlie answered a few perfunctory questions about less important terms. The council thanked him, and he resumed his seat. The councilmen then discussed the matter among themselves at great length. Dad could hear the wall clock ticking behind him. Every twenty or thirty minutes Charlie leaned over and, tapping his wristwatch, whispered in Dad's ear, "When will this be over?" Dad did not reply. They were determined to stick it out to the end. Tonight it would finally be settled—would we or would we not stay in Kansas City? Charlie kept his gaze fixed on the councilmen, alternately smiling and scowling. Sometimes he nodded yes and sometimes no as he listened to the discussion.

Several times Charlie stood up and approached the lectern to clarify something he thought the council didn't have quite right. Each time he did, the tension in the room rose. He did, after all, have a reputation for being impatient and excitable. But thanks to Dad's calming influence, he remained civil.

Much of the council's deliberations focused on Charlie's demand for a new ballpark. With Oakland offering a brand new, and empty, coliseum, would Charlie keep the franchise in Kansas City? They hoped so. They also talked about the possibility of the team's remaining in K. C. *but without Charlie*. He wasn't surprised. *Life* magazine quoted him as saying, "They wanted to starve me out and keep the team." Would Charlie be inclined to sell the franchise to a local group if the city council turned down his proposed terms? Nothing they were talking about was new—these questions had been hashed out ad nauseam for weeks. But until tonight, final agreement had seemed unattainable. Now, as Charlie liked to say, it was time to swing or go take a shower.

Finally, just after 2 a.m., the chairman moved that the city approve the lease with the terms Charlie Finley proposed: two years at $250,000 a year in rent with a promise to build a new stadium. After a long, suspenseful delay, another member seconded the motion. The chairman called for the vote, and one by one the councilmen said "aye." Dad told me he didn't realize he hadn't been breathing while the vote was being taken. He let out a big sigh and looked at Charlie. They beamed at each other. The two of them found a bar open and gulped J&B to celebrate.

The next morning, however, the newly elected city council met, and the first thing it did was tear up the previous night's agreement. All the negotiations had been for nothing. The council demanded five hundred thousand dollars a year in rent and a four-year lease. Charlie, Dad, and the whole Finley family were heartbroken. Somehow Ernie Mehl had "flipped" the incoming members. For us it was the last straw.

By noon Charlie announced that he was moving the team offices out of Municipal Stadium. Under the existing lease, if the offices remained at the stadium past December 31, 1967, a one-year lease extension was automatically triggered. The mayor called Dad offering to extend the cutoff date to January 10, 1968, in hope of further negotiations. Dad passed the message on to Charlie, but Charlie did not return the call.

It was over. We were going to Oakland.

The main reasons Charlie and Dad were ready to go to Oakland were obvious: relentless media vilification, unreasonable rent, and the uncertainty of a new stadium. Another important reason, less publicized, was that the team's television and radio revenue in Oakland would be around a million dollars a year, as compared with fifty thousand dollars a year in Kansas City.[1]

MOVE THE LAWNMOWER—THE FRONT OFFICE IS MOVING IN

In mid-December 1967, Charlie got Dad on the phone. "Carl, we don't have a lease. What do we do with the front office in January?" By the end of the month, everything was boxed up and carted out to several pickups borrowed for the occasion. The solution they came up with was to move the front office to the home of Joe Bowman, a team scout and front office executive, in the suburb of Leawood, Kansas. Dad, Bowman, Hank Peters (the player personnel executive), and their secretaries set up their desks in Bowman's two-car garage and stayed there for seven weeks.

There was only one phone for the house and the franchise office. Bowman recalls, "They used the phone here in the kitchen. [Charlie] got mad when the wife would be talking to her friends. I tried to tell him one day, 'Charlie, you want a telephone that no one's on, you put one in. But as long as that phone is in my kitchen, and my wife is paying for it, she's going to talk on it, and you're not going to tell her how long.' He didn't say any more about it."

The Bowmans soon were exposed to Charlie's unorthodox working hours. When Joe was scouting on the road, his wife received calls from Charlie at one or two o'clock in the morning asking her to find documents in the garage. She usually grumbled but complied. Still, Charlie tried, in his own way, to be considerate, paying for new bluegrass to replace the lawn that his employees trampled.

Sam Gould, the owner of the stadium parking lot, remarked how strange it was to drive by the Bowmans' house and see the whole front office, complete with desks and file cabinets, packed into the garage, the doors usually open to the street.

Dad and Rick Monday moved to Oakland in late 1967 to promote the team's upcoming season, make arrangements for the office's move, and find a stable for Charlie O. The coliseum board had assured the Athletics that the structure would be completely finished in time for the 1968 season, but Dad discovered on his arrival that the walls of the executive offices were still bare cinder block. The board again promised that the offices would be completed, but when the team moved in, the cinder block was still there, giving the executive offices all the charm of a prison cell. After spending a fortune on the stadium in Kansas City with little to show for it, Charlie refused to put any money into finishing the Oakland Coliseum, and the executive office walls were still unfinished when Charlie sold the team in 1980.

▶ ▶ ▶ ◀ ◀ ◀

To this day, Kansas Citians blame Charlie for moving the A's out of Kansas City. But a closer look at the facts shows that Charlie did all he could to stay in town and make the fans happy. He spent half a million dollars to renovate Municipal Stadium in 1961. He pledged $150,000 to lure the Beatles to Kansas City in 1964. He put on every kind of promotion he could think of to draw fans to the ballpark. He pushed MLB to have night games so workers could watch the games. And he gave the team Charlie O as a mascot. He really tried.

The civic and political leaders of Kansas City, especially Ernie Mehl and his newspaper, could have made all the difference. With a little good faith on their part, Charlie Finley and the Kansas City A's probably wouldn't have left.

The bad press continued even after the move to Oakland. On the floor of the U.S. Senate, Stuart Symington of Missouri famously declared that "Oakland is now the luckiest city since Hiroshima." After three

World Series championships, Oakland probably did consider itself pretty lucky.

Ernie Mehl got what he wanted—Charlie Finley was gone from Kansas City. Charlie, for his part, freed himself from uncooperative city authorities and a toxic public relations environment. He headed to Oakland and into baseball destiny.

End of story.

PART II

THE OAKLAND A'S

1968–1982

CHAPTER 14

GAME ON

1968-1969

A fter thirteen seasons in Kansas City, the *Oakland* A's were scheduled to make their debut on April 9, 1968, against Baltimore, and Governor Ronald Reagan was to throw the first pitch. But Martin Luther King Jr. was assassinated on the fourth, and the game was postponed. Reagan threw out the first pitch on April 17 in front of a sold-out crowd of 50,164. Oakland was now an official major-league city (though the Orioles won the game).

The Oakland–Alameda County Coliseum along the Nimitz Freeway in East Oakland had opened in 1966. The financing and construction of the stadium was the work of a private, non-profit corporation led by the real estate developer Robert T. Nahas. When the project was completed, ownership of the Coliseum was transferred to the city and county, though Nahas and the other members of the original corporation (including Senator William Knowland and the industrialist Edgar Kaiser Sr.) constituted the governing board, keeping the day-to-day operations and decision-making power away from the Oakland and Alameda County politicians.

PLAYERS GROW (AND MANAGERS GO)

Rick Monday, the No. 1 pick in MLB's first-ever player draft in 1965, was supposed to be the A's big slugger that first season in Oakland. Charlie and the A's had gotten the first draft pick after finishing the '65 season with the worst record in baseball—59–103—and they took Monday after he had led the Arizona State Sun Devils to the 1965 College World Series championship. After posting a gaudy .359 batting average, Monday was named an All-American and college player of the year. He was so good that he overshadowed his highly touted teammate, the freshman outfielder Reggie Jackson. But Jackson caught the A's front office's eye. A year after drafting Monday, the A's used their 1966 first-round pick to get Jackson, and by the end of the 1968 season he had grabbed the spotlight from Monday.

At the end of the final game of 1968, Bob Kennedy, the A's manager, changed out of his uniform into his street clothes and walked upstairs to the executive offices to meet with Charlie. He was sure that he had done enough to keep his job. In his first year as team skipper, he had led the A's to their best record in sixteen years—not a bad way to start the Oakland era.

A few minutes later, Charlie fired him. Kennedy left the Coliseum without talking to anyone, walking right past the newspaper reporters and even some good friends who had been waiting for him, recalls the Oakland sports writer Ron Bergman in his book *Mustache Gang*. The team's public relations director, Val Binns, followed him and read a prepared statement to the sportswriters, announcing that Kennedy indeed had been let go. His replacement was Hank Bauer.

Hank Bauer was the first manager that Charlie ever hired, replacing holdover Joe Gordon halfway through the 1961 season in Kansas City. Bauer, who was an outfielder for the Athletics at the time, learned of his new job during a game when it was announced over the Municipal Stadium PA system, "Hank Bauer, your playing days are over. You have been named manager of the A's." His first stint lasted through the 1962 season, and now he was back for '69.

The A's first season in Oakland was a winning one: eighty-two wins and eighty losses—a twenty-win improvement over 1967's miserable 62–99 record. Lew Krausse Jr., the hometown Kansas City hero who had shown so much promise in 1961, had a solid season in Oakland. He won ten against eleven losses with a solid 3.11 ERA. His teammate Chuck Dobson, a twenty-four-year-old hurler who had grown up in the shadow of Kansas City Municipal Stadium, went 12–14 with a good 3.00 ERA. The A's were loaded with talent that Charlie and Dad had patiently accumulated, but they were about learn that the baseball seas could be as stormy in Oakland as they had been in Kansas City.

WORKING WITH CHARLIE

In the late '60s someone described the A's as a dysfunctional family. That was a pretty fair comparison. The team and the front office were awash in hurt feelings, and Charlie butted heads with nearly everyone.

Charlie enjoyed a honeymoon with the local press in 1968, but as in Kansas City, it was short lived. When he arrived in Oakland to finalize the move, city leaders were singing his praise. But the shadow of Ernie Mehl stretched farther than anyone expected. He let the Bay Area sports writers know what he thought of the Athletics' ownership before they set foot in California. When it came to the press, Charlie never had a chance.

Dad and Charlie were starting to have disagreements, too, on a number of fronts. For one thing, Dad often believed the players should get a higher salary than Charlie was willing to pay, and he warned him that he risked alienating his top players. Before free agency, the players didn't have much leverage. Holding out at the start of the season was the only way to force an owner to pay attention to a player's salary demands. When this happened, the sports writers were quick to wring their hands, calling it a sign of the times and blaming the "modern ballplayer." In fact, holding out was as old as the double play. Even Joe DiMaggio did it once in the late 1930s. Dad worried that players would hold out or play half-heartedly if they thought they weren't being paid fairly.

Dad recognized that Charlie, like a lot of bosses with a healthy ego, liked an idea a lot more if he thought it was his own. He wasn't the type of guy you told what to do. The best way to persuade Charlie to do something was to not persuade him at all. Dad would start by hinting at something that he thought Charlie should do, gently inserting the idea into a conversation, especially during their daily morning phone calls. "Can you believe what Bill Veeck did for a promotion yesterday?" he'd say, or "I've always been a fan of Billy Williams of the Cubs. A class act and a real Chicago guy." He'd plant the seed and let Charlie's subconscious work it over a bit. Often, in a few days or a few weeks, the idea would become Charlie's "own." As long as he didn't mind never receiving any credit, Dad was a perfect fit that way with Charlie.

The move to Oakland was hard for a lot of front-office employees. With family in Kansas City and deep ties to the Midwest, most of them didn't want to move to a distant, unfamiliar place. A number of them stayed behind, preferring to change jobs than change homes. Carolyn Coffin, who pretty much managed the front office and was especially important to the franchise, did not want to leave Kansas City, but Dad convinced her to come with the team.

Dad himself wasn't sure he would go. But in the off-time after the 1967 season, he looked at his life. He had changed professions, left his hometown and family, and gotten a divorce. He was forcibly estranged from his only child by an ex-wife who was increasingly unstable and erratic. What else did he have in his life except running the A's franchise? So he decided to go to Oakland, but only with several conditions. Charlie had to buy out his minority interest in the franchise, and he had to get rid of his other sports franchises. Charlie agreed.

Dad refocused on the team when the franchise arrived in Oakland in early 1968. Charlie was around less, preferring to run things from his Chicago office or his ranch in Indiana, so he relied on Dad even more to be his eyes and ears around the franchise. Like a lot of wealthy people who came from humble means, Charlie seemed to have a nagging fear that his wealth would be taken from him, which might explain his occasional stinginess. That fear even made Charlie a little paranoid at times, putting more pressure on Dad to ease his concerns. My husband, who got to know Charlie later in life and came to admire him, says, "There are some things about Charlie that we're still trying to figure out."

One of the bigger misconceptions about Charlie is that he cared more about money than winning. Not true. In the early years in Oakland, when Charlie was making nearly all of the player personnel decisions, he burned with the desire to make the A's a World Series winner. The franchise hadn't won a title since Herbert Hoover was president, and the so-called experts thought Charlie's ambition was laughable. But to anyone paying attention to the astonishing level of young talent that Charlie (and Dad) were quietly stockpiling, the idea wasn't so ridiculous.

TARGET PRACTICE

Pitchers started using Reggie Jackson as target practice in the 1969 season. He was hit with a pitch seven times before the All-Star break, including twice in as many games just before the break. Charlie, to his credit, stuck up for Reggie and complained to Cal Hubbard, the American League supervisor of umpires, about the bean balls. Charlie told Hubbard that the pitchers were guilty of a "criminal attack on Reggie."

"As owner of this ball club, I'll be damned if I'll put up with this shit," Charlie told the press. "Jackson has to be protected." Unfortunately, the bean balls didn't stop, as pitchers hit Jackson twenty times during the season, the most in the majors.

The media pressure and the stress of fans' rising expectations put Reggie in the hospital in September with an all-over body rash. The ghost of Babe Ruth had claimed another victim. Reggie would not break any records, failing even to match Ruth's fifty-four homers in a then 154-game season.

Still, Reggie ended the '69 season with a forty-seven homers, third in the league, along with 118 RBIs, a league-leading 123 runs scored, 114 walks, an excellent .410 on-base percentage, and a league-leading .608 slugging percentage.

CHAPTER 15

NEW CITY, NEW BALLPARK, NEW LIFE

1970-1971

After my parents' divorce in 1966, Mom and I had moved back to Dallas. She got a job as a school teacher but soon began a rapid descent into mental instability and financial ruin in which she cut me off from all contact with my father. By June 1970 we had been evicted from our home and were living in a motel. When the manager noticed that Mom seemed depressed and I looked neglected, she called Child Protective Services.

Two days after CPS took me from the motel, Dad showed up with his attorney. I can't describe the joy I felt. It was a miracle. I ran to him and sat on his lap, even if I was now a tall near-teenager. Dad told me that Charlie had said, "Get going and get that little girl here!" I would be living with him now. As we drove to Love Field, I asked him where we were going. "Home," Dad said.

"Where's that?"

"Oakland," he said with a smile. "Oakland, California."

I had just turned twelve, and I never saw my mom again.

We landed in San Francisco and crossed a long silver bridge over the bay to Oakland. I asked where the Golden Gate Bridge was. Dad explained that we were taking the Bay Bridge, which connects San Francisco and Oakland. I said the Bay Bridge looked just as pretty as the pictures of the Golden Gate, yet I'd never heard of it. What was the difference?

"Publicity," Dad said without hesitation. On the drive across the bridge Dad pointed to an island in the bay and told me it was Alcatraz and a lot of Indians lived there. I rolled down the window and inhaled the clean thinly salty air from the bay. It was so fresh and cool! I had never smelled anything like it before, and my stomach tightened up with excitement.

PENTHOUSE LIFE

My new home was at the top of a twenty-five-story luxury apartment building near downtown Oakland. I had gone from a seedy motel to a penthouse suite in a matter of hours! Charlie had leased the apartment, and Dad lived there, running the ball club while Charlie was back in the Midwest. There were three bedrooms—one for Dad, one for me, and the third for Charlie whenever he was in town to check in on the A's. (Dad and I would vacate the apartment when Charlie came.) Looking down from our penthouse perch on the sailboats on Oakland's Lake Merritt, I could see something that was visible only from above—large schools of fish rushing in from the Bay every afternoon. At night to the west I could see the lights of San Francisco and the Bay Bridge. To the east in the Oakland Hills, I could see the spires of the amazing Mormon temple, which looked like a castle to me.

I came to realize that life had so much more to offer than what I had known on the street in Dallas.

Dad had been living a bachelor's life until I arrived. Among the few decorations in the apartment were photos of Harry Caray's family atop the huge television in the living room. The legendary sportscaster, who was in the middle of his one and only season with the A's, often stayed there with Dad and Charlie. Joe DiMaggio used to visit the penthouse when he served as a consultant to the A's in 1968 and 1969. He once cooked an Italian dinner there for Dad, and the two bachelors spent several Friday and Saturday nights together, relaxing and talking baseball.

THE COLISEUM

I couldn't wait to see a home game, but the team was on the road when I arrived in town. I finally got my chance a few weeks later when Dad's girlfriend, Sharon, picked me up on a Saturday morning and drove me to the four-year-old Oakland–Alameda County Coliseum on the southeastern edge of the city. We took a side entrance and walked through an underground tunnel, where it was dark and quiet, in contrast to the commotion and brightness up top.

Dad met us in the reception room of the front office. The walls were ugly gray cinder-block. He said they weren't finished yet, but Oakland had assured us they would be soon. Carolyn Coffin had a desk in the executive office. It was a huge room, which she had mostly to herself, and I could see that she had received quite a promotion for moving to Oakland. Carolyn was the mainstay of the front office. If it weren't for her, Dad told me, the front office would have fallen into chaos.

Carolyn could be tough, and sometimes she butted heads with Monte Moore, our broadcaster, whose office was next to hers. Monte was allergic to strawberries. When Carolyn got peeved with him, she would sneak into his office before he arrived and place a strawberry milkshake on his desk. Dad always managed to remove the milkshake in time.

Dad walked us through the stadium's tunnels and hallways to our box seats, next to the press. These were known then as luxury seats—a small, special section between the second and third decks. This was long before the luxury suites—enclosed rooms with televisions and bar and restaurant amenities—that have become the norm at pro sports games.

I had hoped to sit on the first level, behind the dugout, where other front office employees and players' families sat. But Dad preferred to have us in the luxury seats so he could visit when he popped in to talk with the team's radio announcers, such as Monte Moore, who sat nearby. Dad had a phone in our box seats and another one next to him in the press box so Charlie could call him during games, which he did often.

In ways big and small, I noticed how things were different at the Oakland Coliseum from the Kansas City Municipal Stadium. The Coliseum was drab compared with K. C. Municipal Stadium, which Charlie had splashed with color everywhere. My first visit to the Coliseum was like watching the *Wizard of Oz* in reverse, going from color to black and white.

One thing that was the same was Harvey the mechanical rabbit, ensconced again near home plate, ready to rise from the ground with fresh baseballs whenever needed. The sight of him made me feel at home. But all the other crazy things I remembered from Kansas City were gone. There was no petting zoo with monkeys named after my family; there were no peacocks; there were no dyed sheep behind the bleachers. The only personal touch of Charlie's I could detect was his signature, which appeared before the game on the Coliseum's giant, electronic screen with the message "Charles O. Finley presents the Oakland A's." I searched the field for familiar faces from 1966, that last year I had followed the team, but I found only a few. There was Catfish Hunter, pitcher Chuck Dobson, second baseman Dick Green, and shortstop Bert "Campy" Campaneris. The rest were a lot of young, new faces I didn't recognize.

Another familiar thing missing was summer weather. I felt chilly in the breeze coming off the bay on that June day, and I saw fans in sweaters and windbreakers. The Bay Area's brisk summer winds were strange to me.

PROBLEMS WITH THE NEIGHBORS

Dad and I stayed in the penthouse until the end of 1970, when we suddenly packed up and left in a hurry.

It turned out that Huey P. Newton, the head of the Black Panthers, was living in the suite next to ours. A third suite on our floor was occupied by the FBI, which was very much interested in what was going on in Newton's suite.

My encounters with the Black Panthers were limited to the elevator. Phil Seghi, the A's director of scouting and minor leagues, lived on the seventeenth floor of our apartment building and paid me to walk his poodle, Jacques. One day Jacques and I rode in the elevator from the lobby to the seventeenth floor with three black men in leather jackets. I noticed that they pushed the button for the twenty-fifth floor. I didn't know who lived next to us, and I didn't know who these men were, but they were nice to me. One of them patted Jacques and told me how he wished his dog was as obedient. I rode the elevator with them several more times.

When the Feds learned we lived next to Huey Newton and associates, they approached Dad and Charlie, asking them to gather any information they could. Dad, who had once been a juvenile probation officer and had a cousin in the Dallas office of the FBI, was only too happy to oblige, and he started going through their garbage. Before long, the FBI warned Dad that it was planning a raid on Newton's suite, an operation that would involve breaking down doors. That's when Dad decided it was time for us to move on. Some time afterwards, a newspaper headline read, "Huey Newton, Black Panther leader, busted living lavishly in an Oakland penthouse."

CATCHING UP

As Dad and I settled into our nice yet ordinary new Lake Merritt home, I realized I had missed a lot about the A's first two and a half years in Oakland. I was curious, so I asked Dad to fill in the gaps. I learned that whether the A's were in Kansas City or Oakland, whoever the manager was, whether the team was winning or losing, there were three constants as long as Charlie Finley was the owner—controversy, chaos, and change. Finley's A's were never boring. And, as I was learning, the years 1968 to 1970, just before I was reunited with Dad, had been anything but boring.

Carl Finley (left) with Charlie O. Finley (right) in Kansas City at the Muehlebach Hotel in 1962, discussing terms for Carl to join Charlie in managing the A's.

Author Nancy Finley's mother, from her days as a nurse in the army.

Charlie O. Finley
and Carl Finley
signing a new lease
in Kansas City,
February 1964.

Charlie O entering a barbershop for a shave (1965–1966).

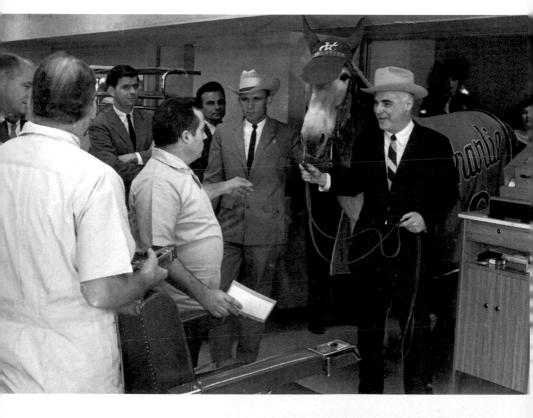

Protests in 1966 in Chicago against the White Sox team for banning the A's mascot, Charlie O the mule.

Miss America Debbie Bryant (from Kansas), throwing a pitch as Catfish Hunter looks on.

Oakland A's player Rollie Fingers deep in thought during a locker room interview (1972).

This illustration of Charlie O appeared on the cover of the 1965 Kansas City A's Yearbook and was used until 1970.

Ticket to an A's 1973 World Series game, featuring Charlie O. The kicking mule was first used in 1971 and became an emblem of the 1970s dynasty.

Author Nancy Finley at an A's game in Oakland Coliseum, August 1973.

Charlie Finley with manager Dick Williams at the 1973 World Series.

Charlie Finley with Alvin Dark, the new manager, at a press conference in January 1974.

Winning game for the 197
World Series, with fans go
wild.

Carl A. Finley (right) with Dr. Thomas Richmond, team physician, in the
Oakland Coliseum press box, August 1978.

Author Nancy H.
Finley with women's
World Series ring (left
hand, middle finger)
commemorating the A's
1972, 1973, and 1974
World Series
wins (1980).

Charlie and the author at his home in LaPorte, IN.

Author's daughter Taylor Finley King's first pitch, April 23, 2003, Oakland Coliseum.

CHAPTER 16

COMING OF AGE IN OAKLAND

1970

A team already brimming with youthful talent welcomed one more exceptionally promising player late in the 1970 season. A twenty-one-year-old pitcher named Vida Blue took the mound against the Minnesota Twins on September 21. After what had been a downbeat month, the A's finally had something to celebrate.

Charlie, however, was disappointed that the team had failed to make the playoffs. It was his tenth season as A's owner, and he had yet to taste any clubhouse champagne. Still, less than a decade after acquiring a franchise that had long been a national joke, his team was now a contender. At the end of 1970, the A's had produced consecutive winning seasons for the first time since 1949, when they were managed by an elderly Connie Mack in Philadelphia. They had finished just short of ninety wins both seasons, and they were still a young team, filled with prospects who were improving every day on the mound and at the plate. But for Charlie the cup was half empty.

During the off-season following the 1970 campaign, Dad reminded Charlie what their former manager Alvin Dark had said in 1967—that the team's bevy of minor-league prospects would bring them to the playoffs in 1971. Would Dark's prediction come true? First, Charlie had to find a new manager, one who would push them over the top and into the playoffs, once and for all.

Dick Williams, who had worked a miracle with the '67 Red Sox but had been fired before the end of the '69 season, spent the 1970 season as the third-base coach of the Montreal Expos, wondering if he would ever get a chance to manage again. But Charlie was keeping tabs on Williams. The team had talent but needed someone to wipe away the three decades of losing that the A's had suffered. Williams had done it in Boston. Could he do it again in Oakland? Charlie thought so.

CHARLIE'S OAKLAND PLAYGROUND

Dad had met his girlfriend, Sharon, two years earlier at an Oakland nightclub. I liked her immediately. She didn't come around the ballpark often. Dad preferred it that way, but she also had her own reasons. She didn't like Charlie—that much was clear. He hadn't made a good first impression on her when he and Dad shared the penthouse in the first couple of years in Oakland.

While Dad and Sharon were starting to date, Charlie and Harry Caray would carouse around town like two sailors on a weekend leave. In a way, that's what they were, these two middle-aged men from the Midwest living it up along the Oakland and San Francisco waterfronts, two thousand miles from home. After they had brought women back to the penthouse high above Lake Merritt, Sharon would come over and find bobby pins and barrettes in the sofa cushions. Charlie was, in Sharon's words, "a player." For my part, I was adjusting to a new lifestyle, getting a PG-version of that Major League Baseball lifestyle that Mom had disliked so much.

In 1971, Dad and Charlie hired attractive young ladies as "ball girls." Their job was to retrieve balls that were foul but didn't leave the field and return them to the home plate umpire. Our first ball girls were Debbi Sivyer and Mary Barry. Debbi's sister, Cathy, was hired to work the switchboard. After her baseball days, Debbi married and, as Mrs. Fields, started selling chocolate chip cookies in Palo Alto. But her first claim to national attention was as one of the famous Oakland A's ball girls.

CHAPTER 17

THE CROUCH BEFORE THE LEAP

1971

I sensed something special was building with this young A's team, if only from the changes I witnessed in Dad. As the season wore on, he became increasingly excited—and he was not an excitable man. I saw him emoting and smiling more, even as the tension grew with the importance of the games.

In 1971, Charlie's intuition in signing Vida Blue paid off. The charismatic rookie had one of the finest pitching seasons in baseball history. Right after he had signed Blue, Charlie attended a game in Oakland and mingled with fans, saying, "Shake the hand that shook Vida Blue's hand!" as though everyone already knew that Blue was someone special. They would soon figure it out.

I liked Vida. He always smiled and was friendly in our front office and at social events. He was perfectly positioned to be baseball's post–Golden Age star—a handsome, gregarious, intelligent athlete who just kept winning. Within weeks, he became a phenomenon, drawing big crowds wherever he went. By some estimates, in fact, one of every twelve tickets sold at American League games around the nation that year was purchased just to see Vida Blue pitch.

Charlie held a "Vida Blue Day" in June, as soon as he recognized that Vida was having a special season. He flew in Vida's mother from Louisiana and gave Vida a baby blue Cadillac Eldorado in a pre-game ceremony in front of a huge crowd at the Coliseum. Charlie owned several Cadillacs of his own, and he considered himself a "Cadillac man." So giving one to recognize excellence was something special in Charlie's eyes.

Vida was generous with the Cadillac, letting his friend and unofficial personal assistant, Spider Hodges—an Oakland jazz musician by night and a construction worker by day—drive the car. When Spider wasn't driving it, Vida also would let the A's teenage clubhouse attendant, Steve Vucinich, take care of it while the pitcher was on the road with the team.

DRESS FOR SUCCESS

On June 27, 1971, any woman wearing the provocative fashion of the day—short shorts known as "hot pants"—was given free admission to a doubleheader between the A's and the Royals at the Coliseum, and the first five thousand fans at the gate got a free bottle of Hot Pants cologne. The promotion was a success, drawing more than thirty-five thousand fans, including about six thousand women clad in hot pants. In between the two games, these women were ushered to the second deck where they sashayed from one foul pole to the other in a type of fashion show while the other fans showed their appreciation.

ALL-STAR BREAK

Reggie Jackson was one of three A's who made the All-Star team that year. On July 13, in the bottom of the third inning, in sold-out Tiger Stadium in Detroit, the twenty-five-year-old Jackson stepped into the left-handed side of the batter's box to face Pittsburgh's controversial Dock Ellis, the National League's right-handed starter. Reggie was pinch-hitting for

Vida Blue, the American League's starting pitcher. Like Vida, Reggie was clad in a uniform that Charlie loved and the baseball establishment loathed—"wedding gown white" shoes, gold socks with green stirrups, a gold helmet, and a white, buttoned jersey with a green "A's" stitched on the front upper right side and the number 9 on the lower left. The jersey was pulled over a green T-shirt with the sleeves cut jaggedly between the elbow and his bulging bicep. Reggie dug those bright white shoes into the batter's box dirt and blasted an Ellis curveball, sending it up, up, and away before it crashed into an electrical transformer atop the second deck in right field. Reggie stopped and stared at it for a few seconds before beginning his trot around the bases.

The monstrous four-bagger was what Bob Costas called "the biggest blast in All-Star history." To the late Ernie Harwell, the Tigers' longtime play-by-play announcer, it was a historic moment in the sport. "That home run Reggie Jackson hit at Tiger Stadium was the hardest hit ball I ever saw," said Harwell. "I didn't think it would ever land anywhere."

The homer started a four-run American League squad rally that led to the AL's first All-Star win since 1962.

It was Reggie's 520-foot blast that everyone was (and still is) talking about afterward. While Vida's superstar season grabbed all the headlines that year—and wore down the young pitcher, who was unaccustomed to fame—a quieter but no less important development for the A's was Reggie's return to superstar form. He swatted thirty-two home runs, batted in eighty runs, and raised his batting average forty points to a solid .277.

The A's other young batters were coming into their own as well. Sal Bando, the team's captain and third baseman, was almost as good as Jackson, hitting twenty-four homers, ninety-four RBIs, and finishing the season with a .271 average. Catfish Hunter was having a great year on the mound. He finished with twenty-one wins and a 2.96 ERA—his best year yet.

In mid-September, the A's were one win away from earning the franchise's first postseason appearance since Connie Mack led the Philadelphia Athletics to the 1931 American League pennant. They closed the deal, finishing with a 101–60 record—the second-best in all of baseball.

THE FIRST CHAMPAGNE

Charlie and Dad were thrilled when the A's division championship finally gave them the opportunity to pop celebratory champagne in the clubhouse for the first time in Charlie's eleven years as owner. Charlie set up American League playoff headquarters at the Edgewater Hyatt hotel on Hegenberger Road, a short distance from the Oakland Coliseum, on the other side of Interstate 880. Charlie O grazed outside the hotel in a specially built pen. Inside, the visiting national sports press ate from a bottomless buffet table of food and guzzled as much free alcohol as they could. There was lobster, ribs, steak, chicken, cookies, salads, beer, and champagne—only the best. Charlie Finley a cheapskate? Not that night.

DISAPPOINTMENT AND PROMISE

Nobody's enthusiasm—not the fans', not the players, not Dad's, not Charlie's—would be enough to topple the Baltimore Orioles in the American League Championship Series. Led by their fiery manager, Earl Weaver, and by twenty-game winner Jim Palmer and several others, the Orioles had too much experience and too much pitching. Baltimore swept the A's in three games.

Despite the disappointment of the early exit from the playoffs, Charlie's brilliant young players were coming into their own. The 1971 season had yielded the success that the team's talent had been promising, tantalizingly, for years. And the man voted MLB's Executive of the Year—Charles O. Finley—had already locked up Dick Williams in a two-year extension a few months before the season ended. Williams would be back for the '72 season. Dad was full of energy, and wore his gentle smile all the time. "Can you believe it?" he asked me. After everything, we were going to be contenders!

The optimism in the air affected Charlie too. If he could run a base-ball team that brilliantly, why not something else? So he decided to expand his realm, acquiring a hockey team—the Oakland Seals—as well as a basketball team. I remember attending A's games during the day and Seals games at night. Dad told me to offer complimentary Seals tickets to my classmates and teachers, but the only one who was interested was my algebra teacher. I ran into him several times at games, smoking a pipe and looking content.

CHAPTER 18

THE SUSPENSE BUILDS

1971

I n the 1960s and early 1970s, there was much hand-wringing about baseball's declining popularity. And as usual, the game's leaders were afraid to do much about it.

Charlie was constantly calling for rule changes that would produce more offense and speed up the game. He called for a designated hitter long before the American League added it. Today the All-Star game is played at night, as are most of the World Series games. Charlie was the first to call for that. "The kids can't see the games in the afternoon," he said. "Neither can the working man in the steel mills or coal mines."

Some of his other ideas went nowhere. For example, he talked about having a designated runner, and he wanted a clock to force quicker pitching, and he wanted baseballs to be a more visible orange. But many of Charlie's ideas were vindicated, despite the initial ridicule by other owners. The first World Series night games were played in 1971. The American League adopted the designated hitter in 1973.

But in the early '60s, Charlie chafed at the torpor of baseball's conservative old guard. "The pathetic, frustrating thing is that all the owners know baseball has slipped, but they don't do anything," he complained. "Baseball faces more competition than the owners realize. Times have changed." A decade later he was still unhappy. *Time* magazine quoted him in 1975 as saying, "I've never seen so many damn idiots as the owners in sport."

Charlie lobbied his fellow owners and the American League's president, Joe Cronin, to try out a new wrinkle in spring practice: the three-ball walk. Employing all the salesmanship for which he was known, Charlie insisted that the innovation would speed up the game and deliver more excitement and higher scores—just the kind of thing needed to capture the attention of younger fans, who were turning to football and rock concerts for entertainment instead of baseball. Just three years earlier, after all, the owners had approved lowering the pitcher's mound with the same goal in mind.

Cronin finally agreed to Charlie's experiment in a spring training exhibition game on March 6, 1971, between the A's and the Milwaukee Brewers. The final score was A's 13, Brewers 9. There were nineteen walks and six home runs—perhaps not surprising, since hitters knew that pitchers had to throw strikes lest they walk yet another batter. There was indeed more offense, as Charlie predicted, but the extra scoring made for a longer game. Within that extended game, however, there was more action on the base paths, and there was a better chance for a team to come back from a big deficit. In other words, there was some merit to Charlie's three-ball-walk idea. But pitchers and traditionalists hated the experiment. It was never tried again, and Charlie was roundly criticized.

READY TO TRY AGAIN IN '72

Charlie had stockpiled four pitchers in his stable who were potential all-stars: Catfish Hunter, Vida Blue, Ken Holtzman, and John "Blue Moon" Odom. Relying on the time-honored principle that you can never have too much pitching, Charlie had ensured that strong starting pitching would return to Oakland even if Chuck Dobson could not come back the following season (he couldn't).

Realizing that his team was on the cusp of greatness, Charlie wanted a new design for their uniforms, one that befitted his future champions. Not surprisingly, he was heedless of tradition. The jersey would be kelly green or "Fort Knox" gold with white numbers, "A's" on the front, and green and gold stripes around the hem of the sleeves. The caps would be kelly green with a gold bill and a white "A's" on the front. The beltless pants would have a green and gold stripe down the side and be worn with white shoes.

Charlie knew he would be criticized for the look, as he had been every year since he first introduced gold-colored uniforms in 1963. He didn't care. "I'm giving them more to snicker over," he said when he unveiled the '72 uniforms.

▶ ▶ ▶ ◀ ◀ ◀

Marvin Miller, the head of the Players' Association—the fairly new but unified labor union representing Major League Baseball players—wanted new terms in the collective bargaining agreement between players and owners. Miller had the full backing of his membership, and they were threatening to strike at the beginning of the '72 season if they didn't get what they wanted. If they went on strike and the season was delayed or (gulp) canceled, it would be a first in MLB history. The players said they were serious. Some of the hard-line owners wanted to call their bluff.

Charlie had finally assembled a team that, despite its stumble in the previous postseason, looked to be a sure-fire winner in 1972. The last thing he wanted was a season shortened or tainted by a needless conflict between the two groups. After a decade of mocking Charlie for doing things his own way, the owners now ignored the insurance expert in their midst as they negotiated with the players over insurance and pensions.

The season was set to start in the first week of April. Would the owners swallow their pride and ask Charlie for the help they so badly needed to save the season from going up in smoke? That would be the intelligent move. But Charlie's experience with his fellow owners had taught him that that crowd could not be counted on to make the smart play.

CHAPTER 19

ANOTHER DIVORCE

1972

T he tension between Charlie and Carl Finley started back in Kansas City, maybe as far back as 1963, when Charlie had to be reminded of his promise to provide our family with a home. The strain increased in 1967, when Charlie was getting ready to move the A's to Oakland and most front-office employees did not want to move with the franchise to the West Coast. Dad didn't want to move that far away either. Dallas would have been convenient for all of us.

Dad had known, of course, that Charlie was in regular communication with Oakland city officials since the early 1960s, but he never thought the move would actually happen. He told Charlie it would "have to be worth my time" to move. Dad had already moved once for the A's, and he had good friends in Kansas City, such as Howard Benjamin.

Once in Oakland, Dad obtained community college teaching credentials in business and industrial management. He eventually got a real estate broker's license and became certified to represent taxpayers before the IRS. Part of the reason he acquired all these credentials was that he liked taking tests, but they also made him less reliant on staying in Charlie's good graces.

Charlie continued to call Dad very early every morning in Oakland as he had done in Kansas City. It was usually about four o'clock when the phone rang. They talked several times per day but Dad's mornings always started with this call. They would discuss just about anything—politics, women, movies, the stock market—but eventually, of course, they got around to talking about baseball and the inner workings of the Oakland A's. Talking to Dad was how Charlie got the inside dope on his team. If there was a labor war brewing in baseball (frequent in those days) or the commissioner was being a pain in the neck (even more frequent) or an important business decision about the ball club had to be made, Charlie knew whom to call. Dad knew it was part of being an A's executive, and over time the calls made him and Charlie closer, despite Charlie's near-constant need to be controlling.

Their work relationship had never been perfect, but Dad was the only man Charlie truly trusted and the only A's employee who had managed to survive the torrent of change in the front office. (Some also said Dad was the only one with enough patience to absorb Charlie's temper.) But Dad thought that Charlie was expecting him to manage the hockey and basketball organizations as well as the baseball team, while he was already over-worked with just the A's. Dad's frustration came to a head during their regular pre-dawn telephone call one day shortly before the start of the 1972 season.

I was doing my homework while Dad talked to Charlie, and I noticed an edge in his voice. The conversation escalated quickly, and Dad did something he almost never did—he screamed. I looked up and saw Dad's face turning red with anger.

"You can't fire me because I quit!" he yelled into the phone.

Dad without the A's? And just four years after he uprooted his life to move with the franchise to Northern California? Charlie's owning the A's without leaning on Dad to run the show? It was hard to say who was taking the bigger risk.

Just a decade earlier, Dad had left his promising career in education to join Charlie and the A's in Kansas City, and the change had proved financially detrimental. After he quit the A's, Dad wrote to a banker friend back in Kansas City about a loan he was having trouble repaying: "I never had problems like this before I entered baseball. In fact, I always paid cash and owed nothing. You can imagine that I would have never left what I had unless I received assurances that my fortune would be much improved. My fortune has been in one steady state of decline."

Without his baseball job and facing mounting debts, Dad went back to education, teaching at a community college near downtown Oakland. He also agreed to a book deal, signing a contract with William Bruns, then an associate editor with *Life* magazine, to write about his life as a baseball man with the Athletics, ending with the move to Oakland. Jim Bouton, an outspoken former Yankees pitcher, had invented the genre of the sports tell-all with his 1970 bestseller *Ball Four*. Until Bouton's book, the press and the players had been discreet about what went on behind MLB clubhouse doors, but Bouton revealed the behind-the-scenes boozing, womanizing, pill-taking, and off-color language indulged in by the titans of America's pastime. He became, in the words of one sportswriter, a social leper in the baseball world.

Would Dad dish the dirt on Charlie and the sometimes-ugly inner workings of Major League Baseball? It sure looked that way as the constant tap-tap-tap of Dad's Smith Corona typewriter sounded through our apartment. Working quietly but persistently on the manuscript throughout that summer of '72, he must have wondered if his "divorce" from Charlie would be as messy as the one from Mom.

For the first time in almost a decade Charlie did not have Dad in the front office taking care of everything. That would take some getting used to. Charlie hired Jimmy Piersall, a former Boston Red Sox outfielder, partly to take Dad's place in the front office. Piersall was as famous for his mental instability as he was for being a two-time All-Star in the mid-1950s. Charlie hired a lot of outcasts over the years, misfits whom the old boys club of baseball owners long had deemed unworthy. The Piersall hire fit that pattern.

Dad was pestered with phone calls from the A's front office and clubhouse, because without him everything was in chaos. It was "Do you know what so-and-so said today?" or, "You won't believe what I have to put up with! Please, please come back!"

But Charlie Finley and the Oakland A's would have to get along without him in 1972.

CHAPTER 20

REDEMPTION

1972

T he 1972 A's season was the kind that baseball fans dream of. They won on Opening Day—a 1–0 nail-biter in eleven innings—lost the next game, and then won eleven of their next fourteen. On May 27, they took first place with a 21–11 record, and two weeks later they had a sparkling 33–13 record. Except for five days in late August, they would not relinquish the AL West division lead. They recaptured first place on August 29 and clinched the division a month later at the Coliseum, defeating the Twins 8–7. A few days later, Ken Holtzman won his nineteenth game, ending the season with a 19–11 record and a sterling 2.53 ERA. Charlie had traded for Holtzman in the winter before the '72 season, and it turned out to be one of his best moves. The trust forged a year earlier by A's manager Dick Williams and his hard-edged players paid dividends. The team stayed focused.

The ball players, of course, continued to fight with each other, recalls the *Oakland Tribune*'s Ron Bergman. "If I wrote a story about clubhouse fights I saw, they'd have to change my beat to boxing." It's hard to imagine a team playing together as a unit, as the A's did, while frequently breaking out in fist fights in the locker room. Dad worried about players injuring each other, but he rarely intervened. "They just need to let off steam," he told me.

The A's also weren't afraid to brawl with the competition. One ugly moment during the summer foreshadowed just how tough the journey to the World Series was to be for the A's. The Green and Gold were playing Detroit at Tiger Stadium on August 21, the first of a three-game series against Billy Martin's Tigers. Detroit pitcher Woodie Fryman beaned Sal Bando, who charged the mound, sparking a particularly nasty brawl between the clubs. There were no serious injuries, but it guaranteed a bitter October showdown between the American League's two best teams.

The A's '72 season is remembered for something in addition to great baseball—the players' facial hair. There are lots of stories in circulation about the origins of the mustaches that became a symbol of the franchise's '70s dynasty, many of them centered on a supposed pre-season faceoff with a newly bearded Reggie Jackson. But the facts are less dramatic. Charlie and Dad had seen an old-fashioned barbershop quartet, complete with handlebar mustaches, singing in a restaurant, and Charlie liked the look. Although Major League Baseball had been completely clean-shaven for sixty years, Charlie offered a three-hundred-dollar bonus to players who grew a mustache. Catfish Hunter and Rollie Fingers accepted the offer enthusiastically, and Fingers's fastidiously curled and waxed whiskers became his lifelong trademark. Other players were more reluctant, but by Fathers' Day—when the A's offered free admission to all mustachioed fans—the entire squad (including Dick Williams) had taken Charlie up on his offer.

THE AMERICAN LEAGUE CHAMPIONSHIP SERIES

The first game of the 1972 AL Championship Series was played in Oakland on October 7. The A's drew first blood, beating Detroit 3–1. Charlie—and everyone else connected to the A's—was jubilant. Billy

Martin was seething. Back at the bar in the Edgewater Hyatt, the hotel near the Coliseum where visiting teams stayed, he grew more incensed with each highball, replaying in his mind key plays from a game he knew the Tigers should have won. Billy didn't just want to win Game Two, he wanted revenge.

By the bottom of the seventh inning, however, Game Two wasn't going Martin's way. The A's were leading by five runs when Bert Campaneris came to bat. He had quickly become a nightmare for Detroit, getting on base four times in eight appearances so far in the series and scoring three of the A's eight runs. The Tigers tried a new way to stop him. The first pitch from the reliever Lerrin LaGrow was a fastball right into Campaneris's ankle, knocking him to the ground. The batter got up, incensed, and hurled his bat at the pitcher's mound, missing LaGrow's head by inches. It took three umpires to restrain an enraged Martin, who charged out of the dugout after Campaneris.

When order was restored, LaGrow and Campaneris had been ejected. Campy's ejection was a formality, as his ankle was too sore to play on for a few days. Though the A's won the game 5–0, they were furious, accusing Martin of ordering LaGrow to hit Campaneris. He angrily denied the charge, but he had once again shown that he was a master at getting inside his opponents' heads. Beaning Campaneris not only removed the slugger from the game—it got the MLB hierarchy involved. The American League president, Joe Cronin, suspended the normally sweet-tempered Campaneris for the rest of the ALCS, and it looked like he might be excluded from World Series as well. In the end, Commissioner Bowie Kuhn suspended him from the first seven games of the 1973 season but not from the World Series. As the teams headed for Detroit, the Tigers were down two games to none and on the brink of elimination. I hoped we could end this ugly series with Game Three.

The Tigers, however, fought back and won Game Three by a 3–0 margin. And in Game Four, they clawed back from a 3–1 deficit in the bottom of the tenth, scoring three runs to stave off elimination to win an October classic by a score of 4–3. The A's, who had been three outs away from winning the series, had blown a two-game lead and were forced into Game Five. The winner would go to the World Series. The loser would be, well, the loser.

Blue Moon Odom took the hill for the A's in Game Five, while Woodie Fryman, whose errant pitch at Sal Bando back in August had incited the enmity between the two teams, started for Detroit. The Tigers scored a run in the first, and the ancient Tiger Stadium shook with the roar of fifty thousand fans. Odom, pitching on just three days' rest, settled down and was stingy over the next four innings. Fryman was even better, but the A's made him pay for every mistake.

In the second inning, Reggie Jackson—then speedy enough to start the game in center field—worked a leadoff walk, stole second, then went to third on Bando's fly ball out to right. Mike Epstein walked and, with men on the corners, Gene Tenace came up to bat. Dick Williams called for a double steal, and like so many of his moves, it worked. Tigers catcher Bill Freehan threw to second to try to nab Epstein, and Reggie sprinted home. He collided with Freehan, barely beating the throw home. The A's had tied the game, but Reggie had torn his hamstring.

In the fourth inning, George Hendrick, who replaced Reggie in the outfield, led off with a grounder to Tigers shortstop Dick McAuliffe, who made an error. Bando sacrificed Hendrick to second, and Tenace singled him home, giving the A's a 2–1 lead. That score held as the Tigers came up to bat in the bottom of the ninth. Vida Blue had relieved Odom in the sixth and had pitched three scoreless innings. Back on the field, Blue got two outs but also allowed a base runner. He and the A's now were one out from winning the series but one bad pitch from heartbreak. Tigers second baseman Tony Taylor stepped in the batter's box. Vida took the sign from Tenace and threw a pitch. Taylor swung and lifted a fly ball to center. Hendrick stood under the ball, watched it drop into his glove, and squeezed.

Just like that, we were going to World Series to face the Cincinnati Reds. Dick Williams and all the players poured out of the dugout and mobbed each other on the field.

Vida Blue, struggling through a mediocre year, had been taken out of the starting rotation and put in relief. At the post-game celebration a fan told me there had been a fight between Odom and Vida Blue in the locker room. Blue apparently remarked to Odom that he fell apart during the game and Blue had to rescue him. The fan said we were an unruly team. "Yes!" I replied, "Isn't it great?"

THE 1972 WORLD SERIES

Oakland's "Swingin' A's" and Cincinnati's "Big Red Machine" would be known as the decade's two best ball clubs. Both franchises had been built painstakingly through excellent drafts throughout the '60s, and their farm systems, aided by a great trade or two, were bearing abundant fruit in 1972. This World Series would go down in history as one of the best, going all seven games and featuring six well-pitched games decided by just one run.

The A's were without Reggie Jackson. Unsung players and surprise heroes would make the difference. One of them was Gene Tenace, who was all the A's needed in Game One. Playing catcher, he helped starting pitcher Kenny Holtzman limit the Reds to two runs, and as batter, he provided all three of the A's runs. He scored the series' first runs by slapping a homer to left of Gary Nolan in the second inning, giving the A's a 2–0 lead. He then broke a 2–2 tie with a solo shot to left in the fifth inning. Rollie Fingers and Vida Blue shut down the Big Red Machine for the rest of the way, and the A's won 3–2.

Game Two went much the same way, featuring that time-tested combination of great pitching and clutch hitting. Starting hurler Catfish Hunter helped his own cause with a single in the second inning, knocking in center fielder George Hendrick. Left fielder Joe Rudi provided an insurance run with a solo homer in the third. The Reds' ninth-inning rally cut the lead in half, 2–1, but it died when pinch hitter Julian Javier swung at a Rollie Fingers pitch and popped out to first baseman Mike Hegan.

The baseball world was in shock. The young, hirsute A's had captured the first two games on the road and headed home to Oakland for three games. The underdog A's suddenly were in the driver's seat.

Game Three was like the first two contests—a tense, close, well-pitched nail-biter that hinged on just one or two key plays. The Reds won, 1–0. Odom was great. The Reds' Jack Billingham was better. He tossed eight shutout innings, surviving two errors from his defense.

Game Four was one for the ages. It symbolized this white-knuckle World Series—a close, dramatic game that featured great pitching, clutch hitting, see-saw scoring, and a one-run margin. After five innings, it felt like a replay of Game One. The A's pitcher Ken Holtzman was dealing a beauty, holding the Reds scoreless and clinging to a 1–0 lead, thanks to a solo homer off Reds ace Don Gullett in the fifth inning by Gene Tenace. That tight score stuck until the top of the eighth, when the Reds chased Holtzman with a rally that reliever Vida Blue could not stop. Both pitchers got tagged with a run and the sold-out Coliseum crowd had been silenced.

It was Reds 2, A's 1, going into the bottom of the ninth inning. As pinch hitter Mike Hegan came to bat to start the frame, the Oakland fans came to their feet, trying to will the hometown nine to a comeback victory. Reds ace reliever Pedro Borbon had other ideas. He retired Hegan. One out. The A's bats—save for Tenace's blast to left—had been quiet all night, knocking just six hits. Now, they were down to their last two outs. Gonzalo Marquez stepped into the batter's box, pinch hitting for George Hendrick, the Athletics' young center fielder. Marquez slapped a single, and the Oakland fans roared. Allan Lewis, a light-hitting but speedy outfielder nicknamed the "Panamanian Express," ran for Marquez. Reds reliever Clay Carroll relieved Borbon to face Tenace. He promptly roped a single off Borbon, and now the A's, though still trailing by a run, had the tying and winning runs on base.

The Coliseum crowd was standing, screaming, and waving the white, green, and gold pennants Charlie had ordered to be given out behind the team dugout. Williams inserted pinch-hitter Angel Mangual, who rose to the occasion. He promptly laced a single, and Tenace ran home and threw his arms in the air and jumped as high as his thick, catcher's legs would allow.

When he landed on home plate, the A's had won Game Four, taking a three-games-to-one lead over the favored Reds. The Coliseum crowd, led by a jubilant Charlie behind the A's dugout, went crazy. While Carroll stared at the grass as he trudged off the field, a sea of A's players swarmed Tenace at home plate.

The Oakland A's now were just one win away from being world champs.

Game Five started out as every A's fan had hoped. With longtime ace pitcher Catfish Hunter on the hill, the sold-out Coliseum was rocking. After three innings, the A's led 3 to 1, and an inning later they led 4 to 2.

The Reds took the lead in the ninth, 5–4, on a Pete Rose single. Meanwhile Sparky Anderson continued to manage as if his life depended on it. The A's got men on first and third with one out in the bottom of the ninth, and Anderson brought in starter Jack Billingham, the Reds' sixth pitcher of the game. Bert Campaneris lifted a high fly ball in foul territory beyond first base. Joe Morgan raced over from second base, caught the ball, and fired it home to nail pinch runner Blue Moon Odom, who had tried to tag up from third base. Instead of celebrating a tying run by Odom, the Coliseum crowd was silenced by Morgan's knockout punch. Cincinnati won the game, and Morgan, without even getting a hit (he had gone 0–3 with two walks and still was batting just .143 in the series), had swung the series' momentum in the Reds' favor.

The teams flew to Cincinnati and played Game Six the next night. The Reds convincingly won 8–1. It was the series' lone game not decided by one run.

Within less than twenty-four hours, the A's had gone from being one or two plays away from winning the World Series to being on the verge of losing it. The series was now tied at three wins apiece.

Uncle Charlie and Aunt Shirley went back to the team's hotel in Cincinnati. Charlie was in a dark mood. He was uncharacteristically quiet, and he could not sleep well after midnight. This is when he called early to talk. It was about two a.m. in California. The phone woke me.

I listened to Dad's side of the conversation. This phone call lasted about an hour.

Charlie was asking Dad what he thought about the player lineup. I felt really good that Charlie was seeking Dad's advice, even though Dad was no longer with the team. Charlie knew that Dad and I would be watching the games. He invited us to attend the postgame party if we won.

With Game Seven just hours away, he knew exactly what was on the line. If the A's won, it would be sweet vindication. The '72 season was his twelfth as A's owner, and Charlie had spent most of that time battling a baseball establishment that loathed and ridiculed him. An A's victory would change the game—on and off the field. Charlie knew the baseball establishment was rooting against him personally as much as they were rooting against his loud green and gold uniforms, his white shoes, his mule mascot, and his mustachioed squad of brawling ball players.

Charlie's young team would be facing a rejuvenated Reds team and their rabid home crowd at Riverfront Stadium. At times like this Charlie almost always called Dad to pick his brain, to talk to a trusted friend, to be reassured, or just to feel a little less alone during a dark day.

Major League Baseball didn't have an Executive of the Year award in 1972. But if it did, Charlie would have won it by a mile. Instead, he'd have to settle for winning the *Sporting News* Man of the Year Award, which in its heyday was a prestigious honor. He had earned it. During the '72 season, he had negotiated more than forty transactions—trades, sales, releases, farm-system promotions and demotions—involving around thirty players. And it was obvious that most of Charlie's deals had worked.

The Reds' Jack Billingham took the mound in front of fifty-six thousand fans at to start Game Seven. Campaneris hit a single but was left on first while Angel Mangual and Joe Rudi were retired. Then the A's caught a bit of luck when Reds center fielder Bobby Tolan misplayed a fly ball by Gene Tenace (playing first base in this game). With the speedy Campy running on contact with two outs, he raced home and scored. After one inning, the A's led 1–0.

When a manager is making a lot of player substitutions, the play-by-play announcer will sometimes say he's "managing this game like it's Game Seven of the World Series." Well, that's how Dick Williams, with good reason, was managing this game. Fortunately, Charlie had loaded the roster with good pitching. Williams would need every last ounce of it.

The A's had a 3–1 lead in the eighth, when Pete Rose laced a single off Catfish. Williams replaced Hunter with Kenny Holtzman—yet another ace pitcher. Holtzman was in just long enough to give up a double to Joe Morgan.

The Reds had the tying run on second with no outs and the heart of the order coming to bat. Williams brought in the A's third pitcher of the inning, Rollie Fingers. The Riverfront Stadium crowd, smelling blood, got up on its feet and roared.

The four A's pitchers who pitched Game Seven had combined for sixty-six of the A's ninety-three wins in 1972. Fingers had won eleven while notching twenty-one saves. The franchise desperately needed one more from him on this night. For the national TV audience, the World Series had been their first glimpse of Fingers, whose waxed handlebar mustache became the enduring symbol for the Swingin' A's and their band of "longhairs." Everyone quickly forgot about his mustache as he got to work, retiring Joe Hague and intentionally walking Johnny Bench to load the bases.

It was a risky move, as putting Bench on first meant that the winning run now was on base, and a double from first baseman Tony Perez could give the Reds a one-run lead with just one inning to go. But the strategy paid off. Fingers got Perez to fly out, scoring Rose and slicing the A's lead in half. They now led 3–2 with two outs and two on. But Fingers put out the fire by retiring third baseman Dennis Menke. The rally was over and the A's were just three outs away.

Fingers took that 3–2 lead into the bottom of the ninth, where he quickly retired the first two batters, Cesar Geronimo and Dave Concepcion. The Reds' final hope was their fifth pinch-hitter of the night, Darrel Chaney. (Sparky Anderson was managing like it was Game Seven, too.) Chaney was one of the weaker hitters on the team. That's why A's fans watching on TV back in Oakland gasped in horror when Fingers plunked him, putting the tying run on first base with Pete Rose coming to bat. Once again, a double with two outs probably would tie the game.

WHITE KNUCKLES

In the stands at Riverfront Stadium, Charlie put his hands together and nervously squeezed them. It was, literally, white-knuckle time. While Dad and I were watching on the big-screen TV at Oscar's, our favorite restaurant in Oakland, Dad whispered his signature "Dammit!" I felt like throwing up. I was old enough to understand almost everything that was going on, but too young to have become philosophical about it. To me, losing this game would be the end of the world.

If anyone was going to be the Reds' hero, it would be Rose. But Fingers was no slouch, either. He waited for Dave Duncan to flash the sign, nodded his head, gave a quick glance to Chaney at first, and then tossed his pitch. Rose swung and lifted a lazy fly ball to shallow left field.

Joe Rudi got under it and made the catch, squeezing the ball into his mitt.

The Oakland A's were World Series champions!

Charlie Finley, the insurance salesman who had been mocked and vilified all these years, now had a team that was the envy of everyone.

I was jumping and skipping among the tables, and Dad just sat there with a huge grin on his face. I could tell he regretted not being part of it. I went to the big post-game party, but Dad stayed home.

Uncle Charlie was the king of the baseball world. In the stands he kissed Aunt Shirley while Williams kissed his wife, Norma. The A's clubhouse was soaked with champagne. The celebratory food, as usual, included lobster, steak, ribs, chicken, prawns, good champagne, beer, pasta, cookies, and crackers with wonderful mystery stuff on top. The food didn't last long.

The players' beards and mustaches were shampooed with a mix of beer and bubbly. The fun continued on the flight back to Oakland.

Charlie loaded the plane with old friends, family, and no shortage of booze, along with the players and coaches. Charlie walked up and down the plane aisles, grinning and singing.

The next day more than a hundred thousand people lined Broadway in downtown Oakland for the victory parade, which ended with the cheering throngs surrounding a stage where the players and Charlie gave speeches to the adoring A's fans.

The World Series title was just as momentous for Oakland and all of Northern California as it was for Charlie. The A's victory was the first major sports championship in Bay Area history. The 49ers, Giants, Raiders, and Warriors had all been playing longer than the A's, but Oakland's baseball team reached the top first. Charlie spared no expense, throwing a huge post-parade party for the players and team employees and their families.

"1972 was my favorite of the three World Series–winning years because it was the first one," said Steve Vucinich, then the A's visiting clubhouse attendant and now the team's equipment manager. "Charlie went all out with the parties, and it was all so new and fun."

CHAPTER 21

RETURN OF THE UNSEEN HAND

1972

When Dad left the A's, Charlie lost more than a key employee. Carl Finley was the unseen hand guiding Charlie's genius. Rarely heard from, he was virtually invisible to fans and the media. He had never played baseball and was content with his career as a high school principal in Dallas when he was plucked from his quiet and comfortable life and thrust into the maelstrom of Charlie Finley's baseball team.

The telephone at our house would ring at five o'clock every morning. It was Charlie calling. Dad would be up with a cup of coffee. Their daily phone call would last anywhere from a few minutes to a few hours. When I was in the room, I could usually tell from Dad's end of the conversation what the topic was. He'd mention players' names, money matters, trouble with the commissioner, team rosters, scouting prospects—the usual baseball subjects. He had a way of planting ideas in Charlie's head. After a few days, Charlie would convince himself that they were *his* ideas and start talking about them. Dad would just smile his little smile, and I knew what was going on.

Dad ran not only the front office, but just about everything other than scouting and meddling with the team. Well, he did meddle a bit, but he did it through Charlie. And a game couldn't begin until he had signed off on the lineup for the day. He had various titles over the years, such as V. P. of public relations, V. P. of ticket management, V. P. of business, including hiring and firing everybody except the team manager. He was the one you talked to when you "talked to the A's." Dad had the Oakland Coliseum's alarm code. Sometimes at home a call would come that the alarm had gone off, and Dad would drive to the Coliseum to check on it. George Toma, the Kansas City Municipal Stadium groundskeeper, who saw and heard everything going on there, recalls, "He ran the complete operation. Today it would take more than a dozen people to do what he did."

A few of the press people noticed Dad's broad range of duties. Ed Leavitt, a columnist for the *Oakland Tribune*, observed that "Charlie sends him where there's the most pressure. People like Carl knock themselves out, and nobody ever hears about them." Mike McKenzie, a sports columnist, called him "Charlie's buffer." David Bush of the *San Francisco Chronicle* called him "the lone front-office guy."

Dad had a talent for smoothing things out. It was not uncommon for Charlie to sweep into town and arbitrarily fire someone, and Dad would hire her back in the morning. In the 1970s Charlie began sending Dad as his representative to the annual MLB owners' meetings, where there was usually lots of smoothing over to be done. Despite his almost universal responsibilities for the franchise, I don't recall the press's ever quoting Dad, who avoided the spotlight. The one they quoted was Charlie.

As I grew older, I came to realize that Dad was the consummate gentleman, but he had a mischievous side as well. He was a card-carrying charter member of the International Order of Dirty Old Men. One of his friends was the "Grand Master," and several of his other (non-baseball) friends were also "officers." His membership card gave the headquarters address as "Franklin at First Street, Oakland, California." A stack of these cards was sitting out when I first arrived at the apartment in Oakland. He quickly hid them, hoping I hadn't seen them, but it was too late. Dad often carried several fake diamond engagement rings in his pocket, and he had fun "proposing" to stewardesses and waitresses. I don't know if any of them took him seriously, but Dad enjoyed his little prank.

CALLING THE INDISPENSABLE MAN

Carl Finley was as close to indispensable as a man can be, and by early December 1972—several weeks since the World Series had ended—Charlie realized it. It couldn't have been later than 4 a.m. when the telephone woke me up. Dad answered, frog-voiced and half-awake.

"I'm sorry, sir, do I have the wrong number?" the caller asked. Dad immediately recognized the voice that had greeted him every morning about this time for a decade. Suppressing a chuckle, Dad played along and answered just as formally: "No, sir, I believe you indeed have the right number."

Charlie then half-jokingly fell back into his old sales technique of capturing the other person's attention by making what sounded like a bold declaration about a fairly trivial topic. He said he believed the state of Indiana had the best ribs—better than Illinois, where he lived; better than New York, and certainly better than California, where he had deigned to telephone his cousin this chilly December morning. Yes, it was clear...the Bay Area in particular couldn't hold a candle to Indiana's food—didn't Carl agree? Charlie asked.

I lay in bed listening to Dad's reply, faintly, through the walls of our apartment: a big belly laugh, a sound that I adored. I always knew everything would be fine when I heard Dad laugh. I smiled, almost reflexively, and dozed off.

When I woke up three hours later, Dad was still on the phone. And he was still laughing, as the conversation had careened into even sillier terrain. Now it was Dad talking about which state had the best beans. (Seriously.) In the two years I lived with Dad before his falling out with Charlie, I had become used to tuning out these calls. And now, as they talked again, I realized I had missed them.

I could tell this phone call had broken the ice, but Dad was a smart man with a long memory, and he would not make the mistake of coming back too quickly or too easily. He remembered the promises Charlie made to him in the early 1960s, promises that took months—in some cases, years—for him to fulfill. When my parents were married, my mom was the heavy, but after the divorce, Dad had to rely on himself to push Charlie for his promises.

First, Charlie obliquely suggested to Dad that he return. He kinda-sorta asked Dad to go back to running the A's front office and everything else in Oakland.

Then he started begging. And Charlie never begged anyone for anything.

Charlie didn't mind being reminded that he had failed to keep a promise. In fact, he liked to see how far he could go without paying a debt. Dad was well aware of this, and now he was vocal about what it would take for him to come back. Dad remained lukewarm, so Charlie upped the ante. He promised Dad a new car (a Chevrolet Caprice convertible), an expense account, and other perks. He also promised a World Series ring and a substantial raise.

"Charlie, I don't want to go through all this again. Do you really mean it this time?"

"Carl, believe me, I really mean it!" There was just one condition: Dad had to agree not to publish his tell-all book.

Finally Dad relented. But the next morning he told Charlie that he had a non-negotiable condition of his own. Charlie had to unload his hockey and basketball franchises and stay focused on the A's. If Charlie didn't know his limits, Dad knew his own, and he wasn't going to run *three* teams. Charlie put up a fight, but Dad stood firm. In fact, firmer than I had ever seen him before. And Charlie had the good sense to realize that Dad was right. Either that, or he was just afraid of losing Dad. In any event, Charlie soon dumped the other franchises. He and Dad stayed fully focused on the baseball team, and with that singular purpose they made baseball history. Pushing Charlie to sell his other teams was probably Dad's most important contribution to the A's dynasty.

Dad was excited to be back at the Coliseum and back with the A's, but he knew Charlie Finley all too well. He continued teaching his evening class at the community college—just in case.

Amazingly, Charlie made good on all of his promises to Dad, and he even presented me with a gold charm engraved "World Series 1972." When Dad saw the new car in the stadium parking lot, he just stood there and beamed. He and Charlie had buried the hatchet once and for all. By the end of 1972, Dad was back in the front office for good. It was as if he never left.

CHAPTER 22

THE A'S RETURN

1973

I f Charlie Finley wasn't a hero in Oakland before the 1972 season, he certainly was after the World Series victory. The championship made people more enthusiastic about Charlie, and it made bearing the Finley name a happier experience for me—for a while, anyway. Some of my schoolmates began asking me what I was doing in an Oakland public school. I didn't know how to respond. Dad, after all, had been a public high school principal, so it never occurred to me to look down on public schools or the kids attending them. When I told Dad what my classmates were saying, he gave me a typically abbreviated response. "Good," he said with a tight smile. He was pleased that people were perplexed and perhaps unconvinced of my relation to Charlie Finley. He was kind of hiding me "in plain sight."

TICKETS

One day I stopped by the Coliseum to say hi to Dad. Charlie was there, and he made me an offer I was too excited about to refuse. I had a new job! With the A's! At the Coliseum! Even Dad didn't try to stop this one. As the A's marched toward another American League Western Division title, I was to help Dad administer playoff ticket sales.

Charlie was growing increasingly mistrustful of anyone but family, and he managed to turn ticket sales into a cloak-and-dagger operation. He had always had a suspicious side, of course. One reason Charlie had hired Dad in the first place was that he wanted a family member he trusted to help him run the ball club. But Dad thought something was different now. He had never seen Charlie so mistrustful of outsiders—he didn't even want security guards hired or the team ticket manager (an otherwise natural choice) involved in the operation.

For security reasons, playoff tickets were processed not at the Coliseum office, where there was plenty of room, but at a vacant bank in San Leandro, a working-class town a few miles south of the Coliseum. For half of August and all of September 1973, that empty bank became our home away from home. Dad and I would get up at 4:30, eat breakfast at the café in the Edgewater Inn, stop at the main Oakland post office to pick up the ticket orders—several sacks full—and arrive at our secret work location by seven or eight o'clock.

AMERICAN LEAGUE CHAMPS

On August 7, baseball took a back seat for the Finleys when Charlie suffered a major heart attack. He spent two weeks in a Chicago hospital then went to recuperate at his LaPorte farm. Meanwhile, the A's went on a tear, leaving their AL West rivals the Kansas City Royals in the dust as they went 21–7 from July 31 to August 31. The A's clinched their third consecutive AL West title after they beat the White Sox in late September, with a still-recovering Charlie in attendance at Comiskey Park.

In the AL Championship series, they faced the Baltimore Orioles, who had their own great stable of arms in Jim Palmer, Mike Cuellar, Dave McNally, and Grant Jackson. Like the Tigers the year before, the Orioles gave the A's all they could handle. Down two games to one, and trailing 4–0 in Game Four, the Orioles staged an incredible comeback.

They won 5–4 and forced a Game Five in Oakland. Baltimore seemed to have all the momentum after shocking the A's the night before. That is, until Catfish Hunter hurled Game Five's first pitch on the evening of October 11. From that point on, it was all A's. Oakland scratched out three runs, including RBIs by Vic Davalillo and Jesus Alou, two of the three players Charlie had picked up in trades on July 31. The third man picked up that day, Mike Andrews, hardly played in the series, going 0–1 with a sacrifice. No matter. Hunter did the rest by tossing a complete game shutout. The A's were back in the World Series. They would face the New York Mets, who had staggered through the '73 season with a .509 winning percentage.

TWO IN A ROW

Game One was in Oakland, and the A's won it 2–1—yet another one-run decision in the World Series. Game Two the following night went twelve innings. In what Curt Gowdy called one of the "longest and weirdest games in World Series history," a blinding afternoon sun made catching flies an almost superhuman feat. Two twelfth-inning errors by Mike Andrews at second base led to three runs and a 10–7 victory for the Mets. Charlie suspected—with good reason, it turned out—that Andrews's errors were attributable to an undisclosed injury, and he had the infielder placed on the disabled list. That decision provoked one of the biggest controversies of Charlie's baseball career and brought down the wrath of Bowie Kuhn, a story told in full in the next chapter.

Game Three, two nights later in New York, was another nail-biter, going eleven innings. The A's won by one run, 3–2.

Many teams crumble under this kind of pressure. Would the A's? The Mike Andrews fiasco dominated the headlines, and the Mets dominated the A's, taking Games Four and Five at Shea Stadium by a combined score of 8–1. The controversy over Game Two had been relentless during the trip east, and it looked like the A's were letting the series get away from them as they returned to Oakland down three games to two. Coming home should have been the perfect tonic for a club just a loss away from elimination. Both teams wanted to get back to focusing on baseball. But the press was treating the Coliseum like a crime scene with Andrews cast as the victim and Charlie, of course, the villain.

Catfish Hunter was the A's Game Six starter. No slouch, he had led the A's in victories and winning percentage in the regular season, notching twenty-one wins against five losses with a 3.34 ERA. He came through on Saturday with a 3–1 win. If the A's were going to win another World Series, it would once again be in Game Seven.

In spite of a week of angry headlines, 49,333 Oakland fans packed the sold-out Coliseum on October 21. They got their money's worth. The A's broke the scoreless tie in the bottom of the third, leaning on the October heroics of a couple of guys for whom it was becoming commonplace. Holtzman started the party by hitting a one-out double. Campaneris did the rest by ripping a two-run homer. A few minutes later, Joe Rudi slapped a single and then Jackson swatted one of his trademark big hits—a high, powerful, no-doubt-about-it shot to the right-field alley that he stopped to admire for a second before jogging around the diamond. Smelling blood, the Coliseum crowd shot to its feet, letting out a primal roar. Within minutes, the A's had raced to a 4–0 lead and now were fifteen outs from being MLB's first repeat World Series winner since the 1962 Yankees. Mets runs in the sixth and the ninth were not enough, and the A's held on to win 5–2—World Series champions once more.

The roar of the Oakland Coliseum reverberated around the East Bay. The team did what most teams do when they win a championship—they hugged and jumped around and poured booze on each other's heads. Charlie congratulated Williams and individual players, but gone was the joviality and the ear-to-ear grin he had flashed in '72. There is video footage of Charlie moving through the clubhouse and walking up to Reggie Jackson, who is surrounded by reporters. Charlie congratulates Reggie, who was named World Series MVP, and Jackson somewhat stiffly thanks him in return. Once Charlie walks away, Jackson flashes a sarcastic look at the journalists hovering nearby. It was that kind of "party."

Unfortunately, there were several reasons for the bad vibes. Bad feelings from the controversy surrounding Andrews lingered, souring the taste of the victory champagne for some players. So did the knowledge that A's skipper Dick Williams was leaving. He had told his squad before Game Six, and they had kept the secret. But now that the season was over, Williams announced that he would not be returning to Oakland the following season.

Some of the players refused to believe it, saying they hoped he'd change his mind. But he didn't. The media, as usual, ran with a story before checking all the facts, splashing it all over the sports pages that he was quitting because of Charlie. But that wasn't true. Although Williams was not a "people person," Charlie had seen something special in him and gone with his intuition. They had made a good pair. But Williams had given Charlie his notice well before the start of the series, and he gave as his reason that he simply wanted to return to the Boston area, which he considered home.

Most of the fans didn't care about the controversies. They lined Broadway in downtown Oakland several deep for the victory parade, just as they had done the year before. The postseason had been as rocky as it was victorious. With two titles under their belt, Dad and some of the players hoped the constant off-the-field controversy would diminish for the Green and Gold. But even more was in store for 1974.

CHAPTER 23

MIKE ANDREWS'S LAST HURRAH

1973

Charlie had suffered a heart attack in August 1973. Watching the second game of the World Series a few months later could not have been good for his condition.

At the start of the twelfth inning, the game tied 6–6, Dick Williams sent his newly acquired designated hitter, Mike Andrews, to cover second base. Why he would put a DH in a fielding position is unclear, but it would be a fateful decision. With the Mets up 7–6, two outs, and the bases loaded, John Milner hit a grounder directly at Andrews. I watched the ball zoom toward him…and then go between his legs! I screamed. Even though Dad was back in the stadium catacombs somewhere, in my mind I could hear him utter his trademark "Goddammit!"

"I don't believe this!" I said to myself. A major league player letting a ball go between his legs—in a tight World Series game! The Mets' lead grew to 9–6.

The next batter hit a grounder that again bounced toward Andrews. In that moment, I felt like throwing up. But I just knew that he wouldn't make another error. He fielded the ball and threw firmly to first base. A routine out. But no, the ball was thrown wide, just enough to pull first baseman Gene Tenace off the bag. The runner was safe, and the Mets' Cleon Jones scored from third. The rest of the game is a blur in my memory. The A's scored once in the bottom of the twelfth but couldn't make up for the three runs that Mike Andrews's errors had allowed.

But the drama on the field paled in comparison with what happened after the game. Charlie, already apprehensive about Andrews's ability to play when he was signed, was alarmed by his two errors and insisted on having him examined by the team doctor, Harry Walker, in the Coliseum. Dr. Walker informed Andrews that he had found something wrong with his right shoulder—biceps tenosynovitis—a condition that often follows a previous injury to an arm or shoulder. He was going to recommend that Andrews be put on the disabled list.

Andrews denied that there was anything wrong with his throwing shoulder. But Charlie's instinct told him that his initial impression about Andrews was correct, and Dr. Walker's report seemed to confirm it. Charlie had Andrews sign Dr. Walker's report, acknowledging his injury, and put him on the disabled list. He reminded Andrew of the time the team bus was departing for the airport in the morning, assuming he would be on the plane to New York with the rest of the team. To Charlie's surprsie, Andrews said he didn't feel like traveling with the team and wanted to go home to Boston. Charlie, trying to be nice, agreed.

Dad considered Andrews's decision a confidential personnel matter, so nothing was said to his teammates. They noticed that Andrews was not on the plane the next day, however, and assumed that Charlie had kicked him off the team. Angry and resentful, the players, led by Reggie Jackson, decided to protest Andrews's supposed ouster by wearing black arm bands.

Two days later Andrews held a press conference and issued a statement accusing Charlie of forcing him to sign a false medical diagnosis in order to put him on the disabled list and make room on the roster for Manny Trillo, a younger fielder, for the remaining games in the series.

Commissioner Bowie Kuhn responded by ordering Andrews back on the roster and fining Charlie. Suddenly Charlie, Andrews, and the whole franchise were embroiled in what the sports writer Bruce Markusen would call "one of the most infamous World Series controversies of all time."[1] Charlie lost the public relations war almost immediately, and to this day he is the official villain in the received narrative of the Andrews affair. Donald Moore's version of the story is typical:

> Little did Andrews know, Finley was going to use him as a scapegoat for the loss, and try to force him off the roster by making him sign a false affidavit claiming he had a shoulder injury. That way, Finley could add the infielder he wanted on the roster in the first place, Manny Trillo.[2]

When Andrews reappeared in Game Four, the Shea Stadium crowd gave him a standing ovation. He grounded out and never played in a Major League game again. Dick Williams was supposedly so disgusted by Charlie's treatment of Andrews and so fed up with his interference that he told his players he was quitting at the end of the World Series.

This retail version is a folk tale largely invented by the press with the encouragement of Kuhn and the perhaps unwitting complicity of Mike Andrews. The media went along with it because the outrageous behavior of a demon owner made a better story than a team led by an insurance salesman and a high school principal winning its second straight World Series.

A FINE CAREER WINDING DOWN

Mike Andrews, always popular with the fans, had had a stellar career with several teams. He began the 1973 season with the White Sox, but his bat had grown cold and his production was fading fast. Just three years after knocking seventeen homers and sixty-five RBIs, Andrews had no homers, ten RBIs, and an anemic .200 average. On July 16 the White Sox released him. Andrews went knocking on doors to see if another team might sign him. Several other teams expressed interest but never offered a contract because of "roster problems." When he finally talked to the A's, Charlie was suspicious that there might be something wrong with him.

He had seen Andrews make a throwing error on television earlier in the season when he was with the White Sox, so he asked Andrews about it. Andrews assured him there was nothing wrong with him. Still, Charlie was not entirely convinced, and he didn't invite Andrews to sign. Instead, he urged him to follow up with the other teams with whom he had been in touch, and if nothing came of it, to get back to him. I think Charlie was hoping Andrews would just go away.

Having been turned down by several teams and out of options, Andrews eventually called Charlie. Caving in to Dick Williams's urging, and against his better judgment, Charlie did him a favor and signed him as a designated hitter. Andrews would have a last chance to be part of a winning World Series team. Dad, like Charlie, had his doubts. I overheard him talking to Charlie over the phone:

"Well, he wouldn't be my first choice, Charlie, but it's up to you."

"And you don't have anyone else for that spot? No one we can call up?"

"I know, it is getting late to go looking. It's your call."

Charlie's qualms were no secret. Andrews later admitted that Charlie told him, "[P]ersonally, I think you're all washed up, but my manager wants you."[3]

THE UNSEEN DRAMA

After Game Two I was wandering the halls inside the administrative quarters. I saw Andrews go into Dr. Walker's office. Then I noticed Andrews, Walker, Dad, and several other front-office people coming and going from Charlie's office, and I heard voices rising and falling.

I didn't think anything about it at the time. I didn't sense that something unusual had happened until about half an hour later. I had gone down to the after-game party, usually a feast. Ordinarily, Dad and

Charlie would come down about fifteen minutes after the game ended to join us for something to eat. But that night, after half an hour had passed, it seemed odd that neither Dad nor Charlie had showed up. Win or lose, Dad almost always came down for the food. Others in the room started asking me what was holding them up. I ran upstairs and saw people still talking in Charlie's office and returned to the party to report the holdup. Finally Dad showed up. He didn't eat anything but said to me bluntly, "Come on. I need to take you home now." We drove straight home, and Dad didn't say anything on the way.

A couple of days later it "hit the fan," or as they say in baseball, a *brouhaha* erupted. Andrews held his press conference, maintaining that Dr. Walker, at Charlie's insistence, had produced a false medical report indicating that Andrews had a disabling condition. He hadn't wanted to sign it, he said, but Charlie had pressured him.

I heard Dad talking to Charlie after Andrews's statement, and he did something unusual—he referred to Andrews as "that son of a bitch." For several decades that's all I knew about the episode. I read the same version of the story as everyone else in books and magazine articles. I assumed that Charlie had made a big mistake.

WHAT REALLY HAPPENED?

Years later, Dad told me what Charlie had told him in that phone call. Andrews tried to trade his signature on the injury report for a contract to play with the A's in the 1974 season. Charlie, by now painfully aware that Andrews was damaged goods, refused. According to Dad, Andrews finally gave in and signed a report that, in Dad's opinion, was a correct diagnosis, and he chose not to seek a second medical opinion. The Andrews controversy thus appeared to be a case of his word against Dad's, and I believed my father. That's where things stood when Dad died in 2002 at the age of seventy-six.

As his health declined, my father gave up his apartment and moved boxes of A's memorabilia and records to my house. I pulled some collector's items from the stash for safekeeping, but for years the stacks of papers and documents sat undisturbed. Eventually, my curiosity moved me to start going through the documents, though I wasn't looking for anything in particular. One day I came across a stack of legal documents that, upon examination, shed new light on the biggest controversy of Charlie Finley's controversial career as owner of the A's.

ANDREWS UNDER OATH

The documents I had found were transcripts of three depositions—statements given under oath in connection with a lawsuit—taken of Mike Andrews. The first deposition, dated February 13, 1976, was given in the case of *Michael Andrews v. Charles O. Finley, et al.* The second, dated June 7, 1976, and the third, dated June 9, 1976, were in connection with a medical board case against Dr. Walker.

The transcripts were full of surprises, and I soon realized that Andrews's testimony gave a very different picture of his dispute with Charlie from the one I'd gotten from the press. To begin with, Andrews disclosed a long history of baseball injuries: a broken ankle in 1963, a hand injury in 1969, an injury to his right shoulder in 1971 (he threw right-handed), and a broken wrist in 1971. The injury to his right shoulder, he said, "only bothered me as far as throwing the ball went, or being active in baseball.... It was just bothering, as I found out, as I would throw." He sought medical attention for that injury, including cortisone injections.

In his examination of Andrews following the second game of the '73 World Series, Dr. Walker expressed concern about "chronic shoulder disability" and told Andrews that he had found something wrong with his shoulder. Such injuries are common enough among professional baseball players, but there is plenty of evidence that Andrews was injury-prone. The sports writer Saul Wisnia notes that when Andrews broke his wrist on September 1, 1971, it was "the fifth time *that year* he had been knocked from a game by injury" (emphasis added).[4]

Several times in the course of the depositions Andrews acknowledged his poor throwing and "erratic arm." He disclosed that in 1972, when he was with the Chicago White Sox, the coaches felt there was something wrong with his throwing and attempted to correct the mechanics of his throwing from second. "[I] never had what you would call an automatic arm, but I managed to get by," he said. He confessed that his performance with the White Sox in 1973 was not good and that in July of that year the team wanted to cut his salary by 20 percent.

In an interview two decades later, Andrews compared his throwing problems to those of several other MLB players, including Chuck Knoblauch and Steve Blass. "They called it 'throwing yips,'" he said. "Nobody knows why it happens but on balls hit right to me where I had a second or two to think about it, I just couldn't make the throw." He referred to that problem in the June 7, 1973, deposition. Asked if he had any type of mental block in connection with releasing the ball, he responded, "Yes. Somewhat." Asked when he thought this difficulty arose, Andrews explained that during the 1973 season he had not played much and was used primarily as a designated hitter.

Q. So you are saying 1973 this difficulty, mental block more or less came about?

A. Yes, I would say it was more substantial in 1973, than it was in 1972.

Andrews testified that he referred to his mental block in a press interview in early 1973 (about one month before he signed with the A's). He had told the reporter, "I am honestly starting to think I have a mental block about throwing. And I have got to do something about it soon." Andrews then made an interesting admission. Referring to his 1971 shoulder injury, he said, "I think as time went on when I was with the White Sox, once a person hurts their arm they become very much aware of not hurting it again...."

The contract that Andrews signed with the A's on August 1, 1973, stated: "The player represents that he has no physical or mental defects known to him and unknown to the appropriate representative of the club which would prevent or impair performance of his services." Yet he admitted in his depositions that he never disclosed to anyone in the A's organization the "mental block" that had become so distressing or the injury to his right shoulder. When a skeptical Charlie Finley had asked Andrews about his condition, the player had replied, "I was perfectly a hundred percent all right." Elsewhere in the deposition he stated, "I told him I was fine and I was ready to play."

In light of this history, Andrews's testimony that he strenuously objected to being examined after Game Two is hardly surprising.

> Q. Were you agitated or upset by the fact of the examination at that time?
> A. Yes.
> Q. Did you express this to Dr. Walker?
> A. Yes, I did.
> Q. What did you tell him?
> A. I told him that I didn't want to be examined; there was no reason for me to be examined.

When Charlie asked Andrews to sign Dr. Walker's report about the condition of his shoulder, he resisted, saying to sign such a document would "be a lie" and would end his baseball career. He insisted to Dr. Walker that "there was nothing the matter with me."

NO NEED FOR A SECOND OPINION

Andrews acknowledged under questioning that Charlie was calm and polite and told him he didn't want him to lie. When the player protested that signing the report would end his career, Charlie told him he didn't have to sign but urged him to do so for the good of the team. Andrews said he finally signed the statement under pressure.

In that meeting with Charlie, Andrews testified, the team owner offered to have him examined by any doctor of Andrews's choosing. He declined the offer, telling Charlie "there's nothing the matter with my arm, and there's no need to see a doctor." He feared that a reported disability would "end" his "promising career."

Asked if he sought a second opinion during the remainder of the World Series, Andrews said no.

> Q. Were you asked to be seen or treated or examined by any physician while you were in New York during the time of the World Series?
> A. No, I had no need to be.
> Q. Had you made any medical appointments, doctor appointments, prior to the time you rejoined the team in New York?
> A. No. I hadn't; I didn't need one.

An experienced professional player who supposedly had just been coerced into signing a false medical report declaring him disabled—a report that would end his participation in the World Series and perhaps his career—didn't seek a second opinion for another three weeks. That's a story that strains credulity.

KUHN INTERVENES

The commissioner of Major League Baseball, Bowie Kuhn, who admittedly had a visceral dislike of Charlie (the feeling was mutual), intervened to keep Andrews off the disabled list. It's hard to believe that Kuhn, overriding an owner's decision that was based on the diagnosis of a respected physician, did not seek a second medical opinion about Andrews's condition. Perhaps a corroboration of the diagnosis would have been too inconvenient. In any case, Andrews's own account of his recent injuries makes Dr. Walker's diagnosis of biceps tenosynovitis more than plausible.

WHO IS THE VICTIM?

Whose fault was the Mike Andrews controversy?

To be honest, Charlie has to share some of the blame. He made the initial mistake giving in to Williams and signing a player about whom he had serious misgivings. Andrews, for his part, concealed his physical and mental problems from both Williams and Charlie. Williams contributed to the disaster by inserting a designated hitter as a fielder late in a tied game. As *Sports Illustrated*'s William Leggett wrote in October 1973, "Andrews has a faulty glove, very limited range and a throwing arm that has been sore for several seasons. Mike Andrews making an error is not a novelty. The fact that Manager Dick Williams had him in the game at second base from the ninth inning through the twelfth was the basic mistake." Andrews, Leggett concluded, was "the wrong man in the wrong place at the wrong time."

CHARLIE GIVES HIM A GIFT

Charlie offered Mike Andrews an opportunity that few ballplayers ever get: to play in a World Series. Andrews also got what most players don't get upon retirement—a standing ovation from the fans, in the *opponents'* ballpark, no less. It was his last hurrah.

In return, Charlie found himself cast as one of the all-time villains of baseball. It's hard to say whether that was Andrews's intention. In my opinion, had it not been for Kuhn's interference, the whole episode would soon have been forgotten in the commotion of another World Series win.

One of the ironies of this story, of course, is that an owner who was so often criticized for "meddling" with his team ended up in this mess precisely because he didn't "meddle." He let Williams' make the decision to sign Andrews and put him in the game at second base. At least Charlie had the last laugh. His team went on to win its second consecutive World Series.

EPILOGUE

Mike Andrews went 0 for 3 with a walk and two notorious fielding errors in the 1973 World Series. He never played for a Major League team again. Today he is the respected chairman of the Dana-Farber Cancer Institute's Jimmy Fund—the signature charity of the Boston Red Sox—where he raises hundreds of millions of dollars for cancer research.

CHAPTER 24

SWITCHBOARD
POLITICS

1973-1974

During high school, I "office-hopped" when needed at the Coliseum. I started hanging out with the switchboard operator in her small office, which had a window with a view of the grandstand's first deck. It was a cozy room, but it was where the action was in the A's offices (outside of the baseball diamond).

It was an old fashioned switchboard like you see in movies. The operator held a cord while answering a call which she plugged into the extension the caller requested. I sat next to the operator one day and watched her deal with the stress of answering the barrage of incoming calls. It was feast or famine—a seemingly endless wave of calls would be followed by a few minutes with no calls at all. In those quiet moments, the operator on duty seemed happy to have someone to talk to. It was a thankless job, with low pay and high stress, so turnover was high.

The close quarters of the switchboard room promoted a feeling of kinship. That little office became almost like a confessional, and the

151

operators told me all kinds of eye-opening stories. I got quite an education just by spending time in that tiny office.

I liked Judy, the third operator I met. She wasn't the smartest person,
but she was friendly. She also was talkative and tended to overshare. She
told me that she was a born-again Christian and, curiously enough, had
just joined the Mormon Church. Unfortunately, she was slow with the
calls coming in, and I had heard that Carolyn Coffin, the office manager,
was planning to fire her. I kept quiet about that, but I had learned how
to work the switchboard, so I offered to help Judy.

When Charlie met new employees, he liked to test them by saying
something off-color or off-the-wall or both. If the new employee was a
woman, he unabashedly flirted. One day Charlie called and introduced
himself over the phone to Judy. After some small talk, I heard Judy telling Charlie the color of her panties. Soon she was breezily answering
what must have been the most intimate and indecent questions. I tried
to look like I hadn't heard anything and buried my head in a notebook,
pretending to study. In the course of this agonizingly long conversation,
Charlie got Judy to reveal just about everything about her personal life.
Finally, he asked to be put through to Carolyn.

About an hour later, Carolyn called Judy in and fired her. Carolyn
had planned it for days, and I don't think she knew anything about
Charlie's conversation with Judy. She told her she could finish her shift
but she wasn't to come back. Poor Judy had one last hope when Charlie
called back. She explained that she'd been fired, and Charlie told her he'd
make sure she could keep her job.

I knew right away this would not turn out well. Carolyn, who had
a strong personality, exercised unquestioned authority within her sphere
and did not need anyone's permission, not even Charlie's, to fire people
in clerical positions. Now he was about to cross that line by overruling
Carolyn on a personnel matter. As soon as Judy got off the phone, she
marched into Carolyn's office and told her that she was not fired "because
Mr. Finley said so." I could hear Carolyn yelling at Judy, ordering her to
leave the Coliseum. Now! At that point I fled to Dad's office and stayed
out of the way. Everyone knew Carolyn would prevail. And she did.

Charlie barely remembered his exchange with Judy, and he never mentioned her again.

Charlie was spending less and less time on the A's operations, but he still called in daily to talk with Dad and Carolyn. If I answered the switchboard when he phoned, he would first tease me by speaking with an Irish or Scottish accent, pretending to be a long-lost relative looking for "those Finleys in baseball." He always made me laugh. But then the conversation would switch to a familiar subject: He wanted to know whether I had read or heard anything about him that day. If I had, he would perk up and want to know every detail. Where did I read it? What was said? Who was the writer? I never wanted to tell him I'd read something negative because I didn't want to make him upset and I didn't want to get the reporter in trouble, but he didn't seem to mind when we discussed critical articles.

Our switchboard operators had a secondary duty. When the phones were slow, they scanned every Bay Area daily newspaper for articles that mentioned Charlie or the team. They would cut out those articles and tape them onto papers placed in a large portfolio. Every month, the updated portfolio was sent to Charlie's Chicago office. He loved to read about himself, even if it was critical.

I continued to work in the switchboard room, getting to know each operator and filling in when she needed a break or called in sick.

DEATH THREATS AND SERIAL KILLERS

One of my more shocking discoveries in the switchboard office was how many death threats the A's offices received over the phone. From time to time, someone—usually a man—would call the A's office and say he was going to shoot a ballplayer. Reggie Jackson once homered during a regular season game at the Coliseum after he had received a death threat. He quickly rounded the bases as his bodyguards anxiously watched from the stands. Most of the time, though, the death threats were reserved for Charles O. Finley. And the number of threatening phone calls increased after his vilification in the '73 World Series. The calls were disturbing enough in themselves, but they became more frightening when a series of violent, but mostly unrelated, events unfolded in the Bay Area.

On November 6, 1973, about two weeks after the A's World Series victory parade downtown, a radical group called the Symbionese Liberation Army shot and killed Marcus Foster, Oakland's superintendent of schools, and seriously wounded his deputy. Within days, rumors emerged that the SLA's preferred target had been Charles O. Finley, who avoided Foster's fate only because they couldn't find him. In fact, Charlie would be hard to find because he was seldom in Oakland in those days. But Dad and I certainly were in town, so Dad pulled me out of school for the rest of the semester and arranged for an independent study program for me at home. "Home," in this case, meant the A's offices at the Oakland Coliseum. I did not return to school until after Christmas vacation.

Then things got weirder.

On February 4, 1974, the SLA struck again in the East Bay, kidnapping the newspaper heiress Patricia Hearst from her Berkeley apartment. At the same time, the police were figuring out that several serial killers were on the loose. The first of more than a dozen random killings in a six-month period—what became known as the Zebra murders—occurred the previous October in San Francisco, just over the bridge from Oakland. Two months later, the future mayor of San Francisco Art Agnos was shot twice in the back after he attended a political meeting in the city's Potrero Hill neighborhood. The bloodshed continued until May 1974, when police arrested seven men in a San Francisco apartment. Four of those arrested were charged and eventually convicted of multiple murders. The killings stopped, and the Zebra case was officially closed.

Around this time I heard Dad and Charlie talking on the phone about "death threats to someone in the Coliseum." No wonder Dad pulled me from school for a spell. I eventually went back to Oakland High and settled back into a routine, but I—and a lot of other people— would remain a little leery about being out in public for too long at one time.

CHAPTER 25

KISS MY ASS

1974

E ver since Charlie snatched the Athletics from under Ernie Mehl's nose at auction in 1960, the sports media had excoriated him as incompetent, rude, crude, and meddling. "There never has been a baseball operation such as this, nothing so bizarre, so impossibly incongruous," wrote Mehl, who denounced Charlie's leadership of the team as "incompetent and bizarre." The insurance salesman's stunning success at building a winning team, however, suggests that much of the criticism was the voice of jealousy.

After making his namesake mule the team mascot, Charlie was fond of saying, "if you want to be my friend, *kiss my ass.*" He thought that was a cute joke. Now, after back-to-back World Series wins, that line was Charlie's response to everyone in baseball who had disparaged him over the years. It expressed his new attitude. He was the winner. They were not.

And he wasn't done yet.

A NEW DARK AGE

Needing a new manager for 1974, Charlie reached into the team's past and hired Alvin Dark, who hadn't donned the Green and Gold since August 1967, when Charlie fired him, re-hired him, and fired him again in the row over TWA Flight 85. The players weren't thrilled by the hire. Dark had developed a reputation for being racially insensitive when he managed the San Francisco Giants in the early 1960s. But the 1974 A's had so much talent and winning had become such a habit that it was difficult to see how they wouldn't win the AL West, at the very least.

Reaching into the past again, Charlie picked up former coach Bobby Hofman, who had been with the team from 1969 to 1970. Then he did something really unconventional. Allan Lewis, the "Panamanian Express," had been Charlie's first designated runner. Charlie had released him after the '73 season, and now he replaced him with Herb Washington, a track star who hadn't played baseball since high school. New manager, new coach, new designated pinch-runner—after the chaos of the previous seasons, the players and fans were used to the trouble and controversy that seemed to accompany everything the Swingin' A's did in the 1970s. So was Dad. Charlie liked it that way.

CLUBHOUSE BRAWL

Then a brawl started. As usual, the A's players weren't fighting the other team, they were fighting each other. Before their game on June 5, Ray Fosse heard a ruckus. In the A's clubhouse, that was nothing new, but this time it was between two of the lineup's stars, outfielders Billy North and Reggie Jackson. Acting on instinct, Fosse ran over and tried to break up the fight. But as fists flew, the peacemaker got the worst of it, suffering a crushed disc in his neck. He was out for three months but returned in September, just in time for the stretch drive and the playoffs. Jackson and North eventually cooled off, but so did their relationship—they warily avoided each other for weeks.

The A's were used to fights, but this one—which robbed them of their starting catcher—left a hangover. The A's won only three games, against nine losses, over the next two weeks. After Boston's Luis Tiant outdueled Vida Blue in a tough 2–1 loss in extra innings, the A's first-place lead shrank to just half a game, and they dropped to a mediocre 34–31 record. Was Fosse that valuable? Or did the players miss Dick Williams that much? It turned out that neither was the case.

The team eventually righted itself, churning out the spurts of W's that these dynasty A's were known for. They won seven of nine games, lost a pair to Kansas City, then won five in a row. They lost a pair to Cleveland but then ripped off seven wins in eight games, pushing their record to 61–42, giving the squad a dominating nine-game lead by late July. It would be that kind of year. Vince Lombardi said that winning was a habit, and the A's—two-thirds of the way through their fourth consecutive division-winning season—had become victory junkies. They just knew how to finish games—not that it had made them any more lighthearted. Sal Bando, the team's captain and third baseman, had little respect for Dark. Ron Bergman reported that late in a game in which Rollie Fingers had put on a few base runners with two outs in the ninth, Dark strolled out to the mound to give Fingers advice. With the rest of the infield joining them on the Coliseum mound, Fingers listened to Dark and nodded his head. But as soon as Dark left, Fingers turned to Bando, "Okay, Sal, what should I really do?" Bando sneaked a look at the batter and muttered, "This guy can't hit a curve; throw him one and let's get out of here." Fingers obeyed his captain and struck the guy out.

A team like the 1974 A's, whose roster boasted several tough, baseball-smart players who'd been playing together for almost a decade, didn't really need a hands-on manager anymore. Their success seemed to be for the good of the group, as opposed to the "individual," as often seen today with free agency. Fortunately, Dark wasn't hands-on or controlling. Even if he had been, A's players—including a handful who didn't care for playing for Dark in the '67 season—likely would have ignored him. Sal Bando once said, "Alvin Dark couldn't manage a meat market." Even though the dig made its way into print, Dark kept writing Bando's name in the lineup card, and the A's kept winning.

Dark may or may not have been able to manage a meat market, but he was proving that he could avoid screwing up a good thing. The A's kept piling up victories. Nearly all the key players were in the prime of their careers. And the team's offensive attack, inconsistent in some years outside of Reggie's heroics, was as balanced as it would ever be.

After each win the entire team would come over to the Edgewater Hotel, which was almost the team's official hotel, for a big party in the restaurant. Usually all the Finleys were there—cousins, great uncles, aunts, etc.—and Dad was in charge. Some of the parties were inside the Coliseum. On those occasions I liked to go down to our "post-party" room and watch our caterers set up decorations and food. If we lost the game instead, we were still expected to show up for the party, so the food didn't go to waste. At some of these parties they brought Charlie O in to share the festivities. I would sneak him some vegetables off my plate. I saw other people doing that too.

THE END OF THE BALL GIRLS

1974 was our final year with the ball girls, Debbi Sivyer (later Mrs. Fields) and her school friend Mary Barry. This unique A's institution was a "very popular innovation of Charles O. Finley's with fans, spectators, players and umpires," according to the team's 1972 yearbook. "It had been traditional to have boys in those positions. Those girls have added chores to their baseball chasing and now even take soft drinks and coffee to the umpires during a break in the game. They wear green hotpants with a gold blouse." But in November or December 1974, Dad told Charlie that he was receiving numerous complaints from our player's wives about the ball girls. I remember Dad telling one of the wives over the phone, "Say no more, I'm calling COF." He explained to Charlie that the girls had to go in the interests of the players' marital harmony, and that was the end of the Oakland A's ball girls.

WORLD SERIES NO. 3 VS. THE L.A. DODGERS

After securing the American League championship in four games against the Baltimore Orioles, the A's faced the Los Angeles Dodgers in the World Series. The opposing teams were both exciting franchises that had built great young teams through rich farm systems. The A's were going for their third consecutive World Series title, yet they were the underdogs. They'd won "only" ninety games and lost seventy-two, while the Dodgers had a dream season, notching 102 wins and sixty losses.

Game One began on October 12 in front of 55,794 people at Dodger Stadium. In a duel between Kenny Holtzman and Andy Messermith, the A's won 3–2.

Game Two was almost identical, only this time in the Dodgers' favor. Vida Blue pitched well enough, giving up three runs after seven innings, including a two-run homer by Dodgers right fielder Joe Ferguson, but Don Sutton gave a masterly performance. Playing in his first World Series, Sutton cruised until the ninth, when he plunked Sal Bando and then gave up a double to Reggie Jackson. Fireman Mike Marshall came in and promptly gave up a single to Joe Rudi, who knocked in two runs. Trailing now by just a run, A's manager Alvin Dark brought in his designated runner, Herb Washington. This was Charlie's moment to shine, for the designated runner was one of his innovations. But because success for Washington meant success for Charlie, many people hated him. Washington was a threat to the "fundamentalist" views of the outraged purists (who are endemic in baseball, then and now).

But Washington wasn't thinking about all that as he took a lead at first. He eyed Marshall and bent his knees, ready to swipe second as soon as he could. Then in a flash Marshall picked him off. Catching Washington leaning toward second, he made a quick throw to first baseman Steve Garvey, who tagged the runner out. The game-tying threat was gone when the A's needed it most. Marshall made quick work of the next two batters, and the Dodgers won 3–2.

In Game Three, the World Series returned to Oakland, with Catfish Hunter on the mound. His superb pitching made up for the A's meager offense, and they won by now familiar score of 3–2.

Game Four, in Oakland, was a rematch of Holtzman versus Messersmith, and the A's lefty got the upper hand by knocking out a homer off the Dodgers ace in the third inning. Then the A's put the contest away with a four-run sixth inning—a veritable explosion given the series' light hitting. Claudell Washington—the A's phenomenal nineteen-year-old outfielder and Berkeley's best ballplayer since Billy Martin in the 1940s— led the way with two hits and a walk. With a 5–2 victory, the A's were just a win away from officially becoming a dynasty.

Win or lose, Game Five would be the season's last in Oakland. If the Dodgers won, the series would head back to L. A. for Game Six and, if necessary, the deciding Game Seven. Game Five pitted two aces against each other: Vida Blue versus Don Sutton, a future Hall of Famer who went on to win 324 games. Sutton had earned nineteen wins in '74, but he wouldn't get one this night.

The nearly fifty thousand A's fans at the sold out Coliseum could smell blood, and third baseman Sal Bando got them going early. He plated Billy North with a sacrifice fly in the first inning. Just an inning later, catcher Ray Fosse got the fans dancing in the aisles with a solo blast to left. Suddenly, the A's were up 2–0, a score that held until the sixth, when a modest rally that included a sacrifice fly by Jim Wynn and a Garvey single tied the game 2–2.

The Dodgers were desperate. Down three games to one, they needed to treat each contest like Game Seven, and Walter Alston managed like it. He brought in Marshall in the sixth, and let the closer go the rest of the way. The following inning, Rudi made them pay for it with a solo homer that electrified the Coliseum crowd. The score was again 3–2.

Rollie Fingers took the hill in the top of the eighth, and Bill Buckner would be the frame's first hitter. The orange October sun was fading, and the shadows began to creep onto the Coliseum diamond. Trailing by a run and down to their final six outs the Dodgers desperately needed a base runner. Buckner hit a single to center field, and what happened next is an underrated part of World Series lore. The A's center fielder, Billy North, simply missed the ball, which rolled behind him toward the outfield wall. Buckner sprinted to second. But then he kept going.

One of the old baseball axioms is that you should never make the first out or the third out at third base. Right fielder Reggie Jackson backed up North, and he ran toward the ball, his back almost entirely turned on Buckner, who made the turn at second base and, his twenty-four-year-old adrenaline trumping common sense, kept running.

Jackson retrieved the ball in right center field and tossed a perfect throw to cutoff man Dick Green, who threw a strike to Bando, who applied a textbook tag to a sliding Buckner at third. Reggie and Green and Bando combined for one of the greatest defensive plays in World Series history because they could rely on each other. Each one knew the other would be there. They just knew.

The Coliseum crowd sprang to its feet when umpire Tom Gorman called him out. Buckner took a second to ponder his mistake—it wouldn't be his last in a World Series—grimacing while kneeling on the infield dirt. The Dodgers' threat was dead, and the A's won the series' fourth 3–2 decision.

In his autobiography, Reggie wrote of the play: "I can throw hard and accurate. But I never even thought of throwing to third. I made the fundamental play I was supposed to make, and it worked. I never even took a look for Greenie before I threw. I threw where he was supposed to be and he was there. I know he didn't look for Bando. He threw where third was and Sal was there."

Reggie thus explains one of the secrets of that A's dynasty. They were so fundamentally sound, in part, because they had played together so long—going back to the mid-1960s, when they honed their skills in minor league barns from Mobile to Modesto to Vancouver. A decade's worth of playing together had given the A's an innate confidence. They knew exactly where the other was going to be, especially when the chips were down. Amidst all the in-fighting and controversy and clutch, highlight-worthy home runs, the truth of the matter is that the dynasty Oakland A's of the '70s won on all the little things that rarely get mentioned because they're not sexy. More often than not, they pulled out a victory on pitching, defense, and fundamentals so strong they didn't even "need to look before throwing."

And that was it. The A's had won the World Series. For the third consecutive time. To this day, that's something only the New York Yankees have ever accomplished. The A's, wearing those loud Fort Knox gold jerseys and wedding gown white pants, mobbed Fingers and Fosse in the infield. Fireworks were set off high above center field, and Oakland's scruffy band of long-haired fans, in full delirium, poured onto the field. It was championship pandemonium at its finest.

Charlie was on top of the baseball world again and, this time he had made history. He had started in 1960 as an outsider, leading the running punchline that was the Kansas City Athletics. Less than fourteen years later, he had beaten the insider's insider, the Dodgers' owner, Walter O'Malley, and reached the rarest of rarified air—three consecutive World Series titles.

CHAPTER 26

CATFISH, THE MILLION-DOLLAR MAN

1975

T he victory champagne from the 1974 World Series had hardly dried on the Coliseum clubhouse floor before Marvin Miller, the head of the MLB Players' Association, persuaded Catfish Hunter to let him file a grievance on his behalf. The complaint was that Charlie, by failing to make an annuity payment of fifty thousand dollars to an insurance company of the pitcher's choosing, had broken his contract with Catfish. Miller and the players' union attorney, Dick Moss, saw this as an open-and-shut case. The contract provided that once Catfish notified Charlie of the breach, the A's had ten days to mend it by making the annuity payment. The ten days had passed with no response from the A's, so the grievance went to an experienced labor arbitrator, Peter Seitz.

Dad told me this wasn't the only time Charlie had been late with a payment. The A's spectacular success, Dad believed, subjected them to higher scrutiny. And Charlie was an insurance man! Dad was a stickler for deadlines—he always called me on January 2 to say he had already finished his tax return—and he tried to caution Charlie about his cavalier attitude.

This was uncharted territory for Major League Baseball. If Seitz ruled against Charlie and the A's, he could penalize them in a number of ways, including making Catfish a free agent. Miller and the players had been seeking free agency for a long time, but the owners had always blocked them. By 1974, the players had grown to hate the Reserve Clause, which they saw as a kind of forced servitude. The former Cardinals outfielder Curt Flood had tried to kill the Reserve Clause in 1970 with a lawsuit attacking the anti-trust exemption that MLB owners had always enjoyed. He got as far as the Supreme Court, which ruled against him in 1972.

Miller saw the dispute between Charlie and Catfish as an opportunity to make free agency a reality. On December 16, Seitz ruled in favor of Catfish and against Charlie. It was official: Hunter was a free agent. For better or for worse, it was a new day in baseball. Many years later, Catfish recalled that he was nervous when he learned about the ruling because he was out of a job. He called Charlie and offered to come back to the A's, but Charlie couldn't afford a free agent Catfish Hunter. So Catfish went out onto the open market. After a bidding war, he signed a five-year contract worth $3.75 million with the Yankees.

The turn of events, from the owners' perspectives, was bad all around. At that point, no one knew what effect the ruling would have on free agency for all ball clubs. But it did affect Seitz, who soon also found himself a "free agent." The owners were so angry over his decision that they fired him as baseball's arbitrator.

Charlie obviously was unhappy too. He had lost his best pitcher, a Cy Young Award winner, and one of his favorite ball players. Oddly enough, no owner had understood the nuances and potential danger of free agency better than Charlie. In fact, he had counseled the other owners that they should make *all* the players free agents because the saturated market would keep the salaries down. Privately, Miller knew Charlie was right, and he fretted that owners might do just that. The result of the ruling, however, was that there was only one free agent, and just as Charlie predicted, the lack of other free agents had started a bidding war that drove up Catfish's salary.

DARK HUMOR

Baseball people in those days often spent the winter months on the banquet circuit, giving speeches at charity events or dinners promoting ticket sales for the upcoming season. In January 1975, Charlie and the A's skipper, Alvin Dark, appeared at a banquet together. It was just a few months after the A's third consecutive World Series victory, and maybe Dark was feeling cocky. While speaking to the crowd, Dark made a joke about Charlie's losing Catfish to free agency. Not smart. The audience half laughed, half groaned, knowing that it might not go over well with the A's owner in attendance.

When it was Charlie's turn to speak, he offered a tight Mona Lisa smile and said, "Managers are a dime a dozen." When spring training started in Mesa a few weeks later, Dark was still the A's manager. But for how long?

A MISERABLE YEAR

As the 1975 season began, Charlie's split-up with his first true star player was official and unavoidable. Unfortunately, it wouldn't be his last divorce of the year.

Aunt Shirley said to me once that Charlie could be "real ornery." That was a nice way to put it. Charlie was always sweet to me, but I knew he had a Scotch-Irish temper. Sometimes he yelled at Shirley. Sometimes he yelled at the kids. I suppose that most dads yell at their kids once in a while, but when Charlie walked into the house, all of his children—my cousins—ran away. That didn't happen in my house when Dad came home. Years later, Charlie told me and a lot of people that he regretted not spending more time with his kids. Whatever finally pushed Aunt Shirley over the edge, she filed for divorce in 1975, and she would never look back.

This may surprise people, but Charlie was genuinely hurt. Though he was not a faithful husband, he wanted to stay married and never would have divorced Shirley. He knew she was a great mother and wife. I do believe that he loved Shirley—though, admittedly, he could have done a better job showing it.

1975 was not a banner year for Charlie Finley. In addition to the divorce, he suffered a heart attack. It was a mild one, but it was a sign that he needed to make some changes. Just a few months earlier, he was on top of the world; a World Series winner again. Now he was in a hospital room, trying to take it easy and make sure he lived to see another baseball season. And, of course, trying to score with his cute nurse.

Divorce, squabbles with Bowie Kuhn, free agency, a heart attack—they all made for a perfect storm of stress for Charlie, and he started relying on Dad more than ever. In February, he had Dad stand in for him in Reggie Jackson's salary mediation proceedings. The team prevailed over Reggie's demand for a salary increase, but Dad told Charlie that he didn't want to act as the team's mediator again, since doing so made his routine work with the players and staff more difficult. The team would need a neutral party for future mediations.

About this time Charlie handed over to Dad one of his most stressful responsibilities: attending the annual MLB owners' meetings. From then on, Dad always attended the meetings as Charlie's representative.

CHAPTER 27

GOING FOR A FOURTH

1975

───────

*Swing hard, in case they throw the ball where
you're swinging.*

—Duke Snider

C harlie talked about celebrating a fourth consecutive title by creat-
ing a World Series ring with a four-leaf-clover design—a leaf for
each championship. But first, the A's had to win it again in 1975.
Charlie's slogan this time was "Keep it alive in '75!"

Dad asked Alexis Paras, who rode our mascot, Charlie O, at A's
home games, to stay with me when he was out of town. I was sixteen,
and Alexis was twenty-one or twenty-two. I knew this was glorified
babysitting, but I liked the company.

Alexis was a "horse person." She took me to a rodeo at the Cow
Palace in San Francisco, where she seemed to know everyone. We walked
around the back, where people were waiting to present a horse or ride a
bull. This was Alexis's world—horses and people who rode horses.

I would go to Skyline Stables with her and watch her prepare Char-
lie O for his presentation. The mule was brushed and his hoofs picked.
Then, dressed in his A's blanket, he was loaded into his personal trailer.
The owner of the stables, Stan Cosca, drove Charlie O to the Coliseum,

while I rode in a separate car with Alexis. Along the way, drivers honked their greetings at Charlie O, and Mr. Cosca drove along with a huge smile on his face.

Once at the Coliseum we led Charlie O out of his trailer and walked him around, making our way to the corridor where Alexis, mounted and ready, waited for the announcer to introduce the mascot, usually fifteen minutes before the game started. Charlie O ran around the perimeter of the field once or twice, took a bow, allowed a few fans to pet him, then trotted back to his stall.

THE SEXIEST BACHELOR IN THE BAY AREA

Dad brought Marcy Bachman to our box at the Coliseum for the night game on the fourth of July. The author of a daily column in the *Oakland Tribune* called "Frankly Female," she was conducting a contest for the ten sexiest bachelors in the Bay Area. I suggested to Dad that Charlie ought to be one of the ten. He was in the midst of a messy divorce, and this would likely lift his spirits. Dad passed the suggestion to Marcy, and in due course Charles Oscar Finley was proclaimed one of the ten sexiest bachelors in the Bay Area. (Marcy kindly ignored the fact that he was a resident of Chicago.) As I had expected, he was thrilled, and after that Marcy could do no wrong.

Charlie had always leaned on Dad in running the team and liked to bounce business ideas off him. But now, emotionally bruised from his divorce, Charlie grew even more dependent on Dad. His neediness took on a different appearance. When Charlie brought a girlfriend to Oakland, he always wanted to know our opinions on her: What'd we think? Was she pretty? Was she funny? Did she get his jokes? Could she hold her own?

In 1975, Charlie had been wealthy for two decades and was an accomplished businessman—practically a household name. In spite of all that, he still had a deep insecurity that drove him to succeed. The '75 A's would need that drive if they were going to get that four-leaf clover.

ALL STAR COLORS

The evening of Tuesday, July 15, 1975, Charlie watched the All-Star Game at Milwaukee County Stadium, where his three-time World Series–winning A's were the most represented franchise. The AL roster boasted seven A's ballplayers—about 25 percent of the squad. The A's had five starters: pitcher Vida Blue, right fielder Reggie Jackson, left fielder Joe Rudi, first baseman Gene Tenace, and shortstop Bert Campaneris. Oakland also had two reserves: outfielder Claudell Washington and relief hurler Rollie Fingers. Catfish Hunter, in his first post-A's season, was there too, now in Yankees pinstripes. Vida and Catfish both got roughed by the NL lineup, and Catfish took the loss.

Never missing a chance to grab the nation's attention, Charlie had A's players wear as many different uniform combinations as possible at the All-Star Game. Some of them wore kelly green tops, some were in Fort Knox gold jerseys, and others donned wedding gown white ones. While most players wore white pants with the various jerseys, at least one player went all-gold.

Commissioner Bowie Kuhn, watching the game alongside Secretary of State Henry Kissinger, must have fumed when he saw the uniform combinations.

ANOTHER PLAYOFF APPEARANCE

Later that day, the All-Star break ended and baseball resumed around the country. For Charlie's Oakland A's, that meant another win. The A's had ended the first half with hurler Ken Holtzman leading Oakland to victory, and on a warm July night in Cleveland, that's how the second half began too. The A's won 6–3, Holtzman notched his twelfth victory, and Oakland led the AL West by nine and a half games. They would not be caught.

The Kansas City Royals whittled their lead down to four and a half games on September 6, but the A's left them in the dust by reeling off ten wins in twelve games, including a seven-game winning streak. They clinched the AL West title on September 24 at the Coliseum with a 13–2 blowout win over manager Chuck Tanner's Chicago White Sox.

It was the fifth consecutive year the A's had tasted champagne after clinching an AL West championship and a trip to the playoffs. While many had predicted the A's would falter without Catfish, the team actually finished with a better record in 1975 than the previous year—98–64, eight wins more than the Catfish-led '74 A's had.

The Green and Gold were still known nationwide as a swaggering, brawling club of hot-headed winners. Glenn Frey of the pop band the Eagles told a *Rolling Stone* interviewer, "We're the Oakland A's of rock & roll. On the field, we can't be beat. But in the clubhouse, well, that's another story." The wins were still piling up, but times definitely were changing. The A's on-field personality shifted in the 1975 season. For the first time in their five-year playoff run, they became a team of sluggers, while pitching stalwarts such as Blue, Holtzman, and Fingers were still playing superbly.

As the A's flew to Boston to face the Red Sox in the American League Championship Series, everyone was aware that no team had won four consecutive World Series championships since 1952, when Casey Stengel's New York Yankees defeated the Brooklyn Dodgers in seven games. Yet the Oakland A's were on the verge of accomplishing the unthinkable. And, as the Green and Gold got ready to play October playoff baseball again on a shadowy fall Saturday in Fenway Park, would anyone be surprised if Charlie Finley's "Mustache Gang" pulled it off?

TICKETS AGAIN

Charlie told me how much he appreciated my help with Dad in the A's office, and as the 1975 American League Championship Series against the Boston Red Sox approached, I was again assigned to the highly sensitive post of ticket processor. That year our secret location was a nondescript one-story office complex on Oakport, across the freeway from the Coliseum.

Once again, Dad and I developed a routine of waking up at 4:30 in the morning and stopping at the Merritt Bakery in Oakland for breakfast. We would reach the office by 6:30 or seven, and I would start opening the envelopes. One thing, however, was different this year—the mail we received from our opponents' fans. Some of the letters were pretty mean, describing in detail what they hoped the Red Sox would do to us. There were threats to "ruin you" and to "put you in the grave"—and those were the polite ones.

Sometimes cash would fall out of the envelopes as we opened them—twenties, fifties, even hundreds. We also received gift certificates and a gold chain. One man wrote asking the person who opened his letter to meet him for dinner. There were occasionally checks from famous people; I recall in particular getting one from Boz Scaggs. Another time, I opened an envelope and a check for thirty-five dollars fell out clipped to an ad for a male anatomical enhancer. It turned out it was addressed to the wrong office.

Charlie's concern that Dad and I might be followed to our secret location developed into a paranoia that I don't recall in earlier seasons. He asked Dad to hire a security guard for a night watch, but then he worried about whether he could trust the guard. Eventually he asked Dad to spend the night with our tickets, which I thought was going too far. Dad spoke to Sergeant Ivey, a retired Oakland policeman and Charlie's bodyguard when he was in the Bay Area, and told Charlie that there would be extra police patrols at night. Charlie was mollified, and Dad did not sleep with the tickets!

CHAPTER 28

FROM THE HIGHS TO THE LOWS

1975

The phone rang at our Oakland apartment on a foggy June morning in 1975. "Carl, it's me," Charlie said, with an extra jolt of energy of his voice. "Meet me at the Edgewater."

This time it was exciting news. *Time* magazine was going to do a cover story on Charlie, and they were sending a photographer that weekend to shoot the photo. Charlie didn't always hit it off with the press, but the magazine's photographer, Fred Kaplan, turned out to be a great guy. He was close in age to Dad and Charlie and was exactly the kind of fun-loving rogue that the Finley boys enjoyed.

The photo shoot was in a warehouse near the Coliseum. As soon as the work was done, Charlie and his twenty-something blonde girlfriend invited Kaplan, who had hit it off with a beautiful brunette stewardess on his flight from New York, to go out with them. They invited Dad and me, too, and the six of us had dinner and drinks at the Fairmont Hotel in San Francisco. I was still just seventeen, but I'm tall, and with makeup I could pass for a decade older than my age. After dinner, Charlie took us to the Tonga Room, a bar at the Fairmont. I felt so grown up hanging out with this crowd, and Charlie, who paid for everything, was a wonderful host, provided that you let him order for everyone. That's how he liked to do things, and you had to go along with the flow.

The issue of *Time* with Charlie on the cover hit the newsstands on August 18 with the headline "Baseball's Super Showman." Wearing a kelly green blazer and cowboy hat and gripping a bat, Charlie glared out from the cover like one of his sluggers staring down a pitcher. The backdrop was alternating rows of white and orange baseballs, a reference to an innovation that Charlie had pushed, unsuccessfully, in 1973. The orange baseball had become a symbol of his devil-may-care approach to the game's hallowed traditions.

The backdrop was my handiwork, actually. *Time*'s concept for the cover called for a stack of orange and white baseballs, but it was up to the franchise to deliver the visuals. That became Dad's responsibility—and thus *my* responsibility. In those days before digital graphic design, we arrived at a low-tech but effective solution: we glued baseballs to a large white poster board. It was that simple. As Charlie gripped a bat and assumed his batter's stance, Dad and I held the poster board behind him while Kaplan snapped away.

Charlie was thrilled with the attention. Catfish Hunter was gone and his wife had divorced him, but to all appearances, Charles O. Finley was on top of the world. His Oakland A's were still the kings of baseball. They had won their third consecutive World Series title just ten months earlier. Now, in the middle of the summer, they were playing great and gunning for a fourth straight championship.

DARK'S BIG MOUTH

Those days should have been the prime of Alvin Dark's managerial career, but he couldn't keep his mouth from getting him into trouble. When Dad read Dark's comment in the *Time* article that "Charlie's tough and rough, and at times you think he's cruel," he put the magazine down on the table and sighed. Though Dark had softened the criticism by adding,

"But he is a winner," Dad knew that wouldn't make up for what Charlie would take as an insult. Sure enough, as Dad and Charlie were winding up their daily phone call on the last Friday of August, Charlie suddenly said, "Carl, did you see what ol' Mr. Dark had to say about yours truly?"

Dad thought he could hear Charlie's teeth grinding. "Forget about it, Charlie, you know how Alvin gets. Especially when he starts talking religion."

"It's one thing if he says it in a small-town, Shitburg, U.S.A., newspaper," Charlie said, getting wound up. "But in a national publication, with millions of readers. I wonder if his God can cure his foot-in-mouth disease."

"It was definitely a stupid thing to say, but that's just Alvin," Dad said. "Do you know how many times he told me I'm going to hell if I don't get closer to Jesus?"

"Jesus? He should concentrate on getting closer to his boss, and not so close to the Chicago White Sox," Charlie said. "I'll forgive him for the quote. Not so much, though, if he comes in second place."

"You'll forgive him for the quote?" Dad asked, genuinely surprised.

"Well ...," Charlie said, pondering the thought. There was a momentary lull, then laughter, from both Dad and Charlie. Forgiveness? "Probably not" was the unspoken thought shared between the two. They'd had so many of these conversations that they could complete each other's sentences. The cousins were still laughing when Charlie hung up the phone.

A few days later, Dark and Charlie were staying at the same hotel. Charlie, who had had a little too much wine, knocked on Alvin's door, told him he was fired, then went back to his room. After downing a couple of shots of his signature J&B scotch, Charlie couldn't remember if he had fired Alvin. So he knocked on Alvin's door again and told him, "Al, you're fired."

"I know," replied Alvin, "you already told me that." In the morning Charlie had forgotten all about firing Dark.

There was one way for Alvin Dark to make amends for his indiscreet comments about Charlie—to win, and to keep winning until the A's had that fourth consecutive World Series title. No franchise had won four championships in a row since the Yankees' five-year streak of 1949–1953. (The Bronx Bombers also had a four-year streak of championships from 1936 through 1939.) Charlie was tantalizingly close to matching the franchise he considered his personal nemesis.

Nobody has done it since. The Boston Red Sox made sure of that.

KING KUHN

During the 1975 season, Bowie Kuhn's contract as MLB commissioner was up for renewal, and Charlie led an attempted revolt against its renewal. Charlie, the Yankees' George Steinbrenner, and a few other American League owners were not happy with Kuhn. He was saved by Walter O'Malley, the Dodgers' longtime owner and the quintessential baseball insider. O'Malley exercised near-complete influence over Kuhn and was not about to lose that power. Working the phones and calling in favors, O'Malley convinced enough owners not to dump Kuhn. The old boys' club took care of its own once again, and the mavericks and innovators were defeated. "When you strike at a king," said Emerson, "you must kill him." A year later, when Charlie wanted to sell off some of his most valuable players, Kuhn would have his opportunity for revenge on Charlie.

THE 1975 PLAYOFFS

The A's finished the 1975 season with ninety-eight wins, taking the AL West by seven games. The first two games of the American League Championship Series against the Red Sox were scheduled for Boston. Games Three and, if necessary, Four and Five would be in Oakland. Charlie attended the games in Boston, but he had told me before the playoffs began that he could not be at Game Three in Oakland. He promised to be at Game Four as well as Game Five if the series went that long. I couldn't remember a time when Charlie was not seated behind the A's dugout during any championship game.

The Red Sox were the underdogs, and for good reason. The A's roster—Jackson, Bando, Tenace, Rudi, North, Fingers, Blue, Holtzman— had become household names, thanks to all those thrilling, tense playoff victories in the previous three Octobers. Boston had talent, but they were young and unproved. Catcher Carlton Fisk was twenty-seven, first baseman Cecil Cooper was twenty-five, and shortstop Rick Burleson was twenty-four. Their All-Star outfield was even younger—Dwight Evans and Fred Lynn were twenty-three, and Jim Rice was twenty-two. They weren't all kids—future Hall of Famer Carl Yastrzemski was thirty-six, and Cuban-born ace pitcher Luis Tiant was—well, nobody really knew how old he was. The press guide said he'd turn thirty-five in a month, but rumor had it he was at least half a decade older.

In Game One at Fenway Park, nobody's age mattered. Boston's youngsters played like savvy vets, and Tiant pitched as if he'd been sipping from the fountain of youth. Boston won 7–1. The A's, meanwhile, looked like they'd been replaced by impostors. Except for Dick Green and Catfish, the core Oakland players were the same, but they didn't play like it. They had more errors (four) than hits (three). Ken Holtzman, who had come up so big for the A's in past playoffs, took the loss, but it was hardly his fault. Five of Boston's seven runs were unearned, thanks to errors by Phil Garner, Sal Bando, Claudell Washington, and Billy North.

At the beginning of Game Two, Oakland fans felt as if things were finally getting back to normal. Reggie Jackson walloped a two-run homer in the first inning, and twenty-two-game-winner Vida Blue silenced the Red Sox hitters. For a while, anyway. After three and a half innings, the Green and Gold led 3–0, and A's fans could exhale, thinking that Game One was an anomaly, a mulligan that that could shrugged off. Then the bottom of the fourth started and all hell broke loose. The Sox tied the game 3–3, with the bulk of the scoring coming on a Yastrzemski two-run homer.

Desperate for reliable pitching, Dark brought in closer Rollie Fingers to start the fifth inning. And the ever-dependable future Hall of Famer was, unfortunately, anything but. Fingers allowed three runs and was tagged with the loss, while Boston's Dick Drago shut down the A's high-powered offense by pitching three scoreless innings. The Sox won 6–3, and thirty-five thousand fans poured out of Fenway knowing they were one win away from heading to the World Series for the first time in eight years.

I was back in Oakland, and like most A's fans I wasn't worried, despite the two resounding losses. Winning in October was what we did, and we fully expected our heroes Reggie, Rollie, Vida, Geno, Rudi, Captain Sal, and the rest of the boys to right the ship. All they needed was a little home cooking and they'd be fine. After all, they had been winning close playoff games for half a decade. Losing was unthinkable.

Two days later, the unthinkable happened in front of 49,358 A's fans who packed the Coliseum. If Alvin Dark was feeling confident, he didn't show it with his choice for starting pitcher. He sent Kenny Holtzman back on the mound to start Game Three on just two days' rest. After a few innings, predictably, the hurler ran out of gas, giving up a run in the fourth and three in the fifth. The Sox went up 5–1.

The A's scored two in the eighth, cutting the lead to 5–3. But we wouldn't score again. That was all she wrote. Boston won the AL Championship Series in a three-game sweep.

ALL OVER NOW

And just like that, one of professional sports' greatest dynasties was over.

I don't remember much from that night, other than taking a deck of cards from Dad's office and playing solitaire after the game as I waited for him to finish his work. Afterward, Dad and I walked out to the car in silence. We drove to Oscar's restaurant, where we knew we would be with friends who would help us drown our sorrows. On the way Dad mumbled, "Sic transit gloria mundi."

"What?" I asked.

"It's an old Latin expression. 'How quickly the glory of the world passes.'"

Everyone—friends, strangers, the bartender—kept trying to console us. "You'll get 'em again next year," or "You guys have won so many, you had to lose some time." They meant well. But at the time, I was inconsolable.

I can't help thinking that one reason we lost the 1975 American League Championship Series is that Charlie Finley was not there. Looking at Charlie's empty seat behind the dugout, it was obvious that the energy was missing. In other games, Charlie would call down to the manager and make a subtle change. This team was like an orchestra playing without the conductor. Whatever alchemy was behind the A's success, Charlie was the one who held it all together. Sure, sometimes he unified the team only because they were all angry at him. Charlie was completely aware of that dynamic. As long as it bred success, he didn't mind at all.

So where was he this time? The chaos of the previous twelve months, especially his messy divorce, had caught up with him. During the series, he had been in Chicago meeting with lawyers and devoting even more time to his insurance business because of the financially precarious situation the divorce might put him in.

Throughout the ALCS and World Series games from 1971 to 1974, players and fans would see Charlie sitting behind the dugout, often with a celebrity like Clint Eastwood, Jack Benny, Bob Hope, George C. Scott, or Miss America. He might join the fans in waving an A's pennant, or he might sit there silently seething at an umpire's bad call. But he was present and accounted for. But this time he wasn't there. And I don't think the unhappy outcome of Game Three was a coincidence.

A few weeks earlier, Alvin Dark had told his church congregation in Castro Valley, a small community about fifteen minutes southeast of the Coliseum, that "if Charlie didn't accept Jesus Christ as his personal savior, he was going to Hell." The comment found its way into the local newspaper and soon became national news. That was yet another negative public comment Dark had made about his boss in less than two years. For Charlie, it was strike three—Dark was out.

Charlie soon set out to hire a new manager. His choice of Chuck Tanner as Alvin Dark's replacement would be one that I would never forget.

CHAPTER 29

THE CREEPING HAND AND STARTING OVER

1975–1976

I t was always exciting to join Dad and Charlie for one of their nights on the town—dinner, a few drinks, and talking baseball and life. On one of these evenings, while we were brainstorming promotions for the A's, Charlie named me a vice president because he was impressed with some of my marketing ideas. I was proud to be recognized, but Dad knew that Charlie was being his usual charming, mischievous self. He let me know gently that, well... he fired me the next morning.

I treasured these times with Dad and Charlie, whether we were at a ballgame in the Coliseum, at a party at Oscar's, or at dinner in San Francisco. The three of us made a family—unusual and offbeat, but a family nonetheless.

Charlie enjoyed those evenings too. He was growing mellower, less restless. The divorce, which had estranged him from his large brood of children, had rocked his world. As rich and powerful as he was, he had never before been this lonely and heartsick, not even when he was deathly ill and hospital-bound in the 1940s. For those who clashed with Charlie in baseball—ex-players, reporters, old managers, fellow owners, and commissioners—it might be tough to envision Charlie as vulnerable. But that's exactly what he was in the mid-to-late 1970s—emotionally, physically, and in time even financially vulnerable.

Before spring training in 1976, Charlie asked Dad to take me out of school and bring me to the Edgewater Hotel for a news conference at which Charlie would introduce the A's new manager, Chuck Tanner. "The press conference will be more educational for her anyway," Charlie said.

Dad agreed, and we met Charlie for breakfast at the hotel a couple of hours before Tanner was to meet the press. While I nibbled on eggs and toast, Dad and Charlie briefly talked about Tanner's personality, his way with people, and his managerial record in Chicago. A little while later, Dad and Charlie disappeared to meet with Tanner, and I waited in the coffee shop.

After an hour, Dad came in to tell me the press conference was about to start. I took a chair toward the back of the huge ballroom, Charlie and Tanner sat at a table at the front of the room, and Dad lingered off to the side. As the silver-haired A's owner and his new manager talked with the press, I realized that I was starting to anticipate certain questions ("How do you manage the modern ballplayer, Chuck?" ... "This is your third skipper in four years, Charlie. What makes you think he'll succeed where others haven't?"). I also anticipated many of the answers. "I don't mind input from Charlie," Tanner said. "He's won three World Series. He must be doing something right." The press conference went smoothly, and Dad and I drove Charlie to the airport in our Camaro.

Tanner was alone in town and knew practically nobody, so Dad and I took him to dinner at Oscar's. He sat between us in a U-shaped booth. I kept quiet while he and Dad talked about the inner workings of the ball club and about life in the Bay Area. Everything was going fine until late in the meal. Then it got weird. Awkwardly, horribly weird.

Suddenly, I felt a hand on my thigh. I was stunned. Keep in mind, I was seventeen, and Tanner was forty-seven. Dad, who had been talking about what to expect in spring training in Arizona, looked at his glass of wine and kept talking, oblivious to what Tanner was doing. I tried my best to keep a straight face, and Tanner kept his eyes on Dad, pretending to listen. I thought for a second that maybe it was just an honest mistake. I moved my leg. But the hand came back. I moved my leg even further away, but his hand again found my thigh.

As Tanner and Dad bantered, I moved my leg again, and for a second it seemed that he had taken the hint. But then there was the hand again, more aggressive this time, moving up my thigh. I quickly grabbed his hand, as if to say, "You are not going any further." Panicked thoughts raced through my head: Do I slap him? Do I scream? Was he just drunk? Do I tell Dad? Or do I do nothing until I have time to think? I chose the latter. Fortunately, dinner was just about over, and I continued to keep Tanner's hand from moving any further.

We drove Tanner back to his hotel after dinner. As he got out of the car, I got out to move to the front seat; Dad stayed in the car. Trying to do the polite thing, I extended my hand to say good-bye to Tanner with a handshake. He grabbed me, pulled me close to him, and tried to kiss me. From the driver's seat, Dad could not see what was happening. I pulled away from Tanner and plunked myself down in the seat next to Dad for protection while the two men said good night.

I was mortified. And even though I knew I'd done nothing wrong, I was embarrassed and kind of ashamed. That's one reason I never told Dad or Charlie what Tanner had done to me. Another reason is that I feared getting Tanner fired and hence jeopardizing the A's chances for success.

Tanner and I never spoke again. He never tried to contact me or find me in the front office, and I was sure to keep my distance. The incident affected me afterwards. I often felt anxious in the company of older men, especially in tight quarters like a restaurant booth. I made sure I sat next to Dad or another woman. All these years later, I wonder if Tanner did the same thing to other young women during his career, which continued until 1988, when he retired from managing at the age of sixty.

STARTING OVER

Meanwhile, some MLB owners and Commissioner Bowie Kuhn were battling Marvin Miller and the MLB Players' Association over the reserve clause and free agency. A dispute involving two players, Dave McNally and Andy Messersmith, went to arbitration, and on December 23, 1975, the arbitrator ruled in favor of the players and free agency. The reserve clause in Major League Baseball was dead.

Charlie and Dad realized that they would probably lose many of their best players, the heart of the roster, to the bidding of other teams, and they had to get busy rebuilding the team. As Charlie had done in the early 1960s, they looked ten years ahead and resolved to "grow" their talent again from the farm team. The first step was to raise money by selling some talent. The A's would conduct a "clearance sale." They had a whole roster of All-Stars, after all, that other teams had long coveted, and Charlie held out for the best possible deals. He realized that he didn't have to trade player for player. He could trade players for cold, hard cash.

On June 15, 1976, Charlie sold Vida Blue for one and half million dollars to the Yankees, who were charging toward their first playoff appearance since 1964, and he sold Rollie Fingers and Joe Rudi to the Red Sox for a million dollars each. In one day, Charlie had raised three and half million dollars, an unprecedented sum for trading players at the time.

By coincidence, Commissioner Bowie Kuhn was in Chicago to watch a White Sox–Orioles game. As soon as he heard about the sales, Kuhn ordered them frozen until he had a chance to review them. First, he called Charlie, who lived and worked in Chicago, and they held a late-night meeting. Charlie pleaded his case, arguing for the deals to be approved. Kuhn said he'd think about it. Marvin Miller again agreed with Charlie, saying that baseball teams had sold players for cash since the sport began, and this was nothing new. While Kuhn deliberated, Fingers, Rudi, and Blue were in limbo—three players temporarily without a franchise. On June 19, Kuhn voided the sales on the grounds that they would be "devastating to baseball's reputation for integrity and to public confidence in the game."

Somehow, through all of the chaos, the A's were still in the pennant race. Though they were twelve games out of first as late as August 6, the proud five-time AL West champs made a gallant effort to capture their sixth consecutive divisional title. With a 1–0 win over the Royals at home on September 28, they shaved Kansas City's lead to two and a half games with four to play. They were close to pulling off a pennant race miracle, but there was no room for error. One loss and they'd be done. The next day they fell to the Royals 4–0, and the A's dynasty went out with a whimper. The Royals celebrated Kansas City's first major league divisional title on the Coliseum grass in Oakland. The A's lost the division by just two and a half games even though Fingers, Vida, and Rudi missed eleven games during the "clearance sale" controversy. If Kuhn had ruled more quickly or had struck a deal with Charlie that allowed him to avoid litigation and keep the players on the field, the A's might have won the division.

As the season ended, the only vets still under contract were Vida Blue and Billy North. Charlie was desperate for cash, complaining that his "scouts had twenty-one players lined up we were going to sign with that money" from the voided sale of Blue, Fingers, and Rudi.[1] Once Charlie got into clearance-sale mode, he saw everyone as a moveable piece. He did something few in baseball have ever done: he traded the manager, Chuck Tanner, for a player—to my relief. Charlie sent Tanner to Pittsburgh for Manny Sanguillen, who would play catcher, first base, and outfield for Charlie's A's.

CHAPTER 30

MORE DEPARTURES

1976-1977

F ew sights are as dreary as a rainy, gray January day in the Bay Area. But Dad seemed especially downcast that day in 1976, less than a month after the Tanner hire, as we walked through the rain to our car after a day of work. The source of his sour mood was the latest defection from the A's organization.

Carolyn Coffin, the team's longest-tenured employee—she'd been there since 1962, a year before Dad came—had given her notice. An astute reader of Charlie's moods, Carolyn was one of the few who could stand up to him and get away with it. She had recently passed the real estate exam and planned to cash in on the state's booming real estate market. I had known her since I was four. Now I was nearly eighteen and was sad to see her go.

Worse, it occurred to me that my over-worked dad would be expected to take on her load as well.

A MASCOT PASSES

The phone rang in Dad's Coliseum office, interrupting a chat we were having about where we would spend Christmas of 1976, which was just nine days away. I had joined Dad at work that day to help out, which I did as often as I could after Carolyn's departure.

Dad stared at the phone as it rang a second time. "That must be Charlie," he said. He picked up the receiver, and I could tell immediately that it wasn't Charlie. Whoever it was had delivered bad news. Dad hung up the phone moments later and paused briefly before turning to me. "Charlie O died," he said. The caller was Stan Cosca, the owner of Skyline Ranch in Oakland, who had been keeping Dad abreast of the beloved mule's failing health.

The Associated Press reported the passing of the A's mascot:

> Charlie O, the Mule and mascot of the Oakland A's, is dead at the age of 20. Charlie O's keeper, Stanley Cosca, said he died peacefully of a liver ailment at the University of California-Davis Veterinarian Clinic Wednesday evening. "He was tremendously loved," said Cosca, owner of the Skyline Ranch in Oakland and Charlie O's caretaker during his nine-year career with the A's. "He made so many people, so many children happy." Charlie O was hospitalized on Dec. 8, Cosca said, and when word spread of his illness, baseball fans of all ages sent get well cards.

When Dad read the story, he noted with annoyance that Charlie O's career with the A's had actually lasted twelve years. The mule's three years in Kansas City were important because that's where he started. Dad could be a stickler that way; it was the old school teacher in him coming out. But he was unhappy for another reason as well: Dad and Charlie had been dissatisfied with Stan Cosca for a while.

When the team came to Oakland, Dad was eager to demonstrate the A's loyalty to their new hometown, and housing Charlie O in the city seemed like a nice gesture. Someone recommended Skyline Ranch, and

Stan's assurance that he had experience with mules was all Dad needed to hear.

For half a decade, it was a great arrangement. Stan took good care of the A's mascot and did a fine job whenever he brought Charlie O to the Coliseum for one of his many visits. But after a while, Dad started hearing rumors about Stan. In 1974, a reporter told him he'd heard that Stan was using the mule for events not related to the A's , including Stan's son's wedding. Dad didn't like that, and he knew Charlie wouldn't like it either. The A's were paying for Charlie O's stabling, food, grooming, veterinary care, and transportation, and he didn't think Stan should use the A's famous mascot for other purposes.

There were other complaints. When A's fans learned where Charlie O was boarded, they would drive to Skyline Ranch to visit him. Dad and Charlie thought that any fans who went to the effort to visit Charlie O should be able to see him, but there were reports that Stan was turning them away. Dad also heard a rumor that Skyline Ranch had charged a fee for some fans to see the mule. If this was true, where was that money going?

In time, Charlie and Dad started making surprise visits to Skyline Ranch whenever Charlie was in town. Dad and I would pick him up at the airport and go directly to the ranch for an inspection. I remember the look on Stan's face when we drove up—startled, like a deer caught in the headlights. Stan would drop everything and tell his wife to make us a meal, then the three men would sit down for a few drinks and a bite. On the way home from the stable, Dad and Charlie would laugh about Stan's nervous hospitality, but Charlie was worried. He was accustomed to people's getting flustered around him because of his reputation, but something about Stan's behavior alarmed him. As early as 1974, Dad and Charlie were voicing concern about Stan, wondering if he was becoming possessive of Charlie O. "Stan needs to understand that he's only boarding Charlie O, he doesn't own Charlie O," Charlie said to Dad one night over a steak at Oscar's.

When the mule died in late 1976, Dad knew that fans would be nearly as sad as he and Charlie were. Charlie was in Chicago, so he asked

Dad to handle the mule's interment. Dad, as usual, made a sensible choice, selecting the Oakland SPCA, practically next door to the Coliseum, as Charlie O's resting place. The mule had once appeared on the cover of the SPCA's brochure and had occasionally made charity appearances for the organization. Charlie O was cremated, and his ashes were deposited behind a wall inside the SPCA. Joining his ashes were his green and gold blanket, A's hat, and reins. The mule's convertible trailer was donated to SPCA. For a time during the '76 season, A's fans could stop to pay their respects. We made sure this option was announced in print ads and that Monte Moore announced it during game broadcasts.

It wasn't only fans who missed Charlie O. Upon his induction into the National Baseball Hall of Fame in 2009—years after both Charlies, the man and the mule, had gone to their rewards—Rickey Henderson recalled how Charles O. Finley, the antic if parsimonious A's owner, called him up to Oakland in June 1979. "Charlie, wherever you at, and that donkey, I'd like to say thank you for the opportunity."

To this day, I still get asked, "Whatever happened to Charlie O?" His ashes remained at the Oakland SPCA for many years. Today, I have the ashes in an urn in a huge safe in a secret place.

CHAPTER 31

TRIALS AND TRIBULATIONS

1976-1977

For Charlie, the months between 1976 and 1978 were about rebuilding the A's for the future. Charlie's and Dad's early morning phone conferences were about prospects and the future. There was talk of trades, as well. Before free agency sent the price of players' contracts soaring, none of the trades was intended to bring the A's a profit. Charlie and Dad focused on how the farm team and good trades could improve the team's skill and talent on the field.

Dad cautioned me not to say anything about what he and Charlie were doing to rebuild the team. The reason was simple—they were sick and tired of the unrelenting vilification of the sports media, and they didn't want to have to put up with reporters trying to stoke up some news about Charlie's team management. They were also preparing to settle a score with Bowie Kuhn.

FINLEY V. KUHN

Charlie was still enraged by Kuhn's decision to block his sale of several players during the 1976 season. He believed the commissioner had overstepped his authority, blocking routine transactions out of personal animus toward Charlie.

Charlie never backed down from such a fight. He filed a lawsuit against Kuhn in federal district court in Chicago, seeking ten million dollars in damages and taking their feud to heights rarely seen in sports. Nobody could recall an owner's suing an MLB commissioner before, but if the lawsuit was unprecedented, so was Kuhn's interference. So Charlie's and Kuhn's biggest battle yet would be settled in a packed Chicago courtroom.

The trial in *Finley v. Kuhn* began December 16, 1976, with Judge Frank McGarr presiding, and lasted several weeks. There were two issues: Were Charlie's sales truly not "in the best interest of baseball," as Kuhn had claimed, and had Kuhn acted improperly when he blocked the deals, overstepping his authority as commissioner?

Charlie testified that he would have spent the three and a half million dollars that Kuhn denied him to keep his unsigned players, to add other teams' free agents to the A's roster, to replenish the farm team, and to pay the franchise's ongoing expenses. Neil Papiano, Charlie's attorney, called witnesses who described Connie Mack's famous "fire sales" with the Philadelphia Athletics, in which he had sold players for the 1977 equivalent of four and a half million dollars. There were several other instances of owners selling players for handsome sums, just as Charlie had done, with no interference from the MLB commissioner. Why, then, had Kuhn gone against precedent and blocked Charlie's sales?

Kuhn liked to depict himself as the game's protector. On the witness stand, he actually called himself, "the conscience of the game." He argued that Charlie's "big cash deals" would have upset baseball's "competitive balance" and were unfair to Oakland baseball fans. Less than a year later, Kuhn would show how much he really cared about Oakland fans when he tried to help Charlie sell the A's to Denver oilman Marvin Davis, who had plans to move the club to Colorado. In trying to give the entire Bay Area market to the San Francisco Giants—who had been underperforming on and off the field for a decade—Kuhn suddenly didn't seem to care much about "fairness" to Oakland and East Bay sports fans.

The sportswriter Jerome Holtzman attended the entire trial. Fifteen years later he recalled the farcical nature of much of the testimony:

> [T]here was a parade of 20 witnesses, 13 for Kuhn, seven for Finley. I knew them all, except for a Northwestern University economics professor. This gave me an edge. I knew who was telling the truth....
>
> It was my first trial, and what surprised me was that all but two or three of the witnesses for Kuhn were constantly fudging. I was naive. Once the oath was taken, I thought, everyone told the truth and nothing but the truth. I was in Arizona covering the Cubs when McGarr's decision was announced in mid-March. By coincidence, a day or two later one of the club executives who had testified for Kuhn had come to Mesa for an exhibition game. I said to him, "You guys didn't tell the truth."
>
> I have never forgotten his response:
>
> "Of course we didn't. We were co-defendants. We wanted the commissioner to win."[1]

The trial ended January 13, 1977, and, while McGarr was preparing his ruling, Charlie fired another salvo in this ongoing battle: he sold a player for a lot of cash. He dealt middle reliever Paul Lindblad to the Texas Rangers for four hundred thousand dollars, a deal that, predictably, Kuhn tried to block. Charlie then fought Kuhn's stay on the Lindblad sale. It made for a strange and awkward battle, as both sides once again lawyered up over an issue which a federal judge was already trying to decide. Charlie stepped up the war of words, telling reporters that he had essentially told Kuhn "to go to hell." As Kuhn scrutinized the Lindblad sale, Charlie famously declared, "Before, I called this man a village idiot. I apologize to the villages across the country, I should have said he's the nation's idiot." Perhaps fearful of looking bad in the eyes of the judge, Kuhn invented a solution with no precedent. He allowed the sale of Lindblad but placed an arbitrary cap on player sales of four hundred thousand dollars—the price, coincidentally, of the Lindblad deal.

Judge McGarr issued his ruling in *Finley v. Kuhn* on St. Patrick's Day—March 17, 1977—in favor of Kuhn. "The question before the court is not whether Bowie Kuhn was wise to do what he did, but rather whether he had the authority," he wrote. Under MLB's arcane rules, the commissioner's power is "broad and unfettered...to prevent any conduct destructive of the confidence in the integrity of baseball." Charlie appealed the district court's decision but lost again.

PREPARING FOR SOMEDAY

As the 1977 season began, only two players, Vida Blue and outfielder Billy North, were left from the "three-peat" World Series teams, and only a few other names were recognizable to the casual fan. Manny Sanguillen had arrived in the Chuck Tanner trade with Pittsburgh, a historic manager-for-player deal after the '76 season. In the winter, Charlie and Dad had added a fourth recognizable name—Dick Allen, a slugger who had starred for the Phillies throughout the 1960s and for the White Sox in the early '70s. Thirty-five and in the twilight of a fine playing career, Allen had a reputation as a rebel, but that didn't scare Charlie, who understood rebels. Allen embraced the A's custom of putting players' first names or nicknames on their jerseys, one of Charlie's many innovations that annoyed baseball's old guard. Allen put "Wampum" on the back of his uniform, a reference to his hometown of Wampum, Pennsylvania.

Allen became the subject of a series of disagreements between Charlie and the A's new manager, Jack McKeon. "To be a productive player, I would have [Allen] in the line-up five days a week," McKeon recalled decades later. "Charlie wanted him playing every day and reminded me how much he was paying Allen ($100,000)."

Charlie could stomach a strong-willed manager who had an impressive record, as the leeway he gave Dick Williams showed. But he had little patience with a manager who was difficult *and* didn't win very much. So he fired McKeon after only fifty-three games, one-third of the way through the season, replacing him with third-base coach Bobby Winkles. The A's finished in seventh place—dead last in the American League West, just a year after barely missing the playoffs. 1977 was the A's first losing season since 1967 and their first ever in Oakland. The fans stopped coming, and attendance at the Coliseum fell to only 495,599 that year.

For fans accustomed to winning World Series titles, it was a terrible time. But looking at the '77 roster with the benefit of hindsight, anyone can see that Charlie was stocking the A's with talented young players who would become stars, just as he had done when he purchased the franchise in 1960. Tony Armas (age twenty-three), Mitchell Page (twenty-five), and Rick Langford (twenty-five) joined Mike Norris (twenty-two), Matt Keough (twenty-one), Steve McCatty (twenty-three), and other raw youngsters who someday would strike fear in the hearts of opponents. But the '77 season was not quite that someday.

CHAPTER 32

DON'T LET THEM!

1977

The phone rang inside a Coliseum office where Dad worked. It was Charlie. That wasn't unusual—Charlie called every morning. But something was wrong. Charlie shouldn't have been calling anyone. He was in a hospital and scheduled to have heart surgery in a few minutes. Even more alarming, Charlie was slurring his words.

"You okay, Charlie?" Dad asked, trying to sound calm. "You're in the hospital, right?"

Yes, he was, dammit, Charlie explained. Somehow, while lying on a gurney in an operating room, Charlie had fought off the anesthesia and convinced the nurses to give him a desk phone for one last call before going under the knife.

Dad placed his forehead in his palm as he heard the rest of the tale. Gone was Charlie's authoritative, deep voice. He sounded stressed, scared, almost panicked. "Don't let them take my team, Carl!" he bellowed into the phone. "They're trying to take it from me. Don't let them!" Charlie's panicky tone made Dad tense. He wondered who "they" were.

In reality, Charlie had no reason to worry. Whatever he needed, Dad would take care of it. Dad always took care of it, however difficult or outlandish "it" was. "Taking care of it" had been Dad's job in the A's front office for almost fifteen years.

"It's going to be okay, Charlie," Dad said in a soothing, measured tone. "They'll never take the A's from you. I won't let them. You hear me. Charlie, it's okay. I'm here for you. We're *all* here for you. Okay?" Dad shot me a look and flashed a tight smile.

"Now how about you put the phone down and let those pretty little nurses do their job and get you feelin' better?" he said softly. "Good man. I'll call you when you wake up." With that, Charlie faded to sleep. Dad hung up the phone and we both exhaled. Everything was going to be all right.

Charlie liked talking to anybody about this operation, even Kuhn. "Not only did he tell me in detail about his operation but he showed even livelier interest in describing his beautiful nurse who, he said, was sitting on his bed. Indeed, Finley, who revealed his Lotharian reputation, insisted on having her talk to me. She was charming."[1]

DENVER DALLIANCE

Back in Oakland, Dad and I would drive from our place in Alameda to work at the Coliseum. Since Carolyn Coffin had left the A's in early 1976, Dad's workload at the team's Coliseum office had grown even heavier. He had a new secretary, but was she fairly useless, so I helped Dad at the office as much as possible. By now I was taking college courses, so my schedule was flexible.

We usually arrived about eight o'clock and were always the first ones at the office. Dad would turn on all the lights and deactivate the alarm. Everyone started his day by stopping at Dad's office to say hi. The switchboard operators had to be there by nine. Dad's secretary was always one of the last ones to arrive, which drove me crazy.

In 1977, Charlie actually thought seriously about moving the team out of Oakland. Bowie Kuhn, for obscure reasons, was urging Charlie to sell the franchise to the oilman Marvin Davis, who wanted to bring an MLB team to Denver. Charlie first sent Dad to Denver to explore the possibilities and later sent Steve Vucinich, our visiting clubhouse manager, to explore further.

One morning about ten, I was working in the Coliseum switchboard room when I got a call from Steve Vucinich, calling from Las Vegas. I put him through to Dad. "So, what's the word, Carl?" Vucinich asked. "Are we the Denver A's or, or what?"

"Well, Voose, you know the way to Oakland, right?" Dad said, coyly.

"Yeah?" Vucinich said. "Is that where I'm headed?"

"I'll see you at the Coliseum tomorrow," Dad replied.

"So, no deal, huh?" Vucinich said. "The Marvin Davis thing is dead."

"The *Oakland* A's have a lot of work to do before opening night," Dad said, once again emphasizing a particular word. "In *Oakland.*"

Vucinich got off the phone as quickly as possible and told his crew. They were headed home. To Oakland.

The drama of the A's front office versus the Coliseum board continued. After almost a decade, the franchise's offices still hadn't been finished out, and we worked inside cinderblock walls. This is one reason Charlie looked to Denver in 1977. He was trying to scare some sense into the Coliseum Board. Charlie was fond of the saying "Fool me once, shame on you, fool me twice, shame on me." He remembered the money he had put into renovating Memorial Stadium in Kansas City without any reimbursement from the city. To add credibility to his threat to move, he sent Dad to Denver.

The franchise felt unappreciated in 1976 and 1977. After so many wins, there was the feeling we were still not loved. Far from it.

CHAPTER 33

THE LAST STRAW

1977-1978-1979

T hree thousand miles east of the Coliseum, there was proof that Charlie had not lost his ability to spot a winner. The player was still just a teenager, but he combined brilliance on the diamond with the confidence and roguish eccentricity that the Finley boys loved. Ricky Henderson would become the greatest leadoff hitter of all time and Oakland's next Hall of Famer. Charlie had drafted and signed him in 1976, weeks after his high school graduation. Now he was playing outfield for the Jersey City A's, Oakland's double-A farm team.

To the trained eye, there was hope on the horizon. Charlie was rebuilding the farm system, and all those young players—Henderson, Tony Armas, Dwayne Murphy, Rick Langford, Mike Norris, Brian Kingman, Mike Morgan, Matt Keough, Steve McCatty, Bob Lacey, and others—were raw, but their potential was undeniable.

Charlie wanted to remain owner, but certain realities had to be faced. Free agency had been around for nearly half a decade and was not going away. Neither was Aunt Shirley's divorce judgment. If he sold the team now, with its fortunes at a low ebb, it would be a steal for the lucky buyer. No, if he was going to sell the franchise he needed to hire a manager who could resuscitate the franchise and do it quickly. He needed a manager to squeeze as many W's as possible out of that roster of raw, young talent. He needed someone to stir up excitement with the fans and get them to the Coliseum.

But who?

As was his custom, Charlie sent Dad to represent him at the 1977 annual owners' meeting in Chicago and to be his proxy for any votes. But this time Dad was there on a secret mission. During a break in the meeting, he invited some people over to the hotel bar. Joe DiMaggio was seated next to him, along with Whitey Ford and Billy Martin. Dad seems to have used the opportunity to suggest to Martin that he come to Oakland and manage the A's. Martin was noncommittal but clearly interested. By the end of the meeting, Dad had convinced him to come to work for the A's in 1980.

Despite this coup, Dad was getting burned out by this time. In his morning phone conferences with Charlie, he started suggesting that it was time to sell. But Charlie wasn't ready, so Dad backed off and let Charlie's subconscious work on him.

CHARLIE IN LOVE

In 1979, to almost everyone's surprise, Charlie announced he had a new girlfriend. Her name was Susan, and he was clearly smitten with her, and she appeared smitten with him as well. He flew her on the Concorde to Europe for a month's vacation. Charlie sent Dad and me a postcard from their hotel in Oslo: "Dear Carl & Nancy—Enjoying a good vacation. On my way to Stockholm. Love, Charlie." For Charlie, that was the equivalent of giddy.

Charlie and Susan were an item for several months. Just knowing that he had someone to hug and kiss made all of us a little happier. But I don't recall ever hearing her last name. When he brought her to visit us in Oakland, Charlie pulled me aside and asked me what I thought of her.

I gave my usual reply to that question—very pretty, smart, and friendly. He beamed. Then he wandered over to Dad and asked the same question. I could see Dad give his little smile as they talked. Charlie beamed again.

Charlie's romantic life was not without its risks. One evening in 1979, he was sitting with Susan at a bar in Chicago when a man came up and whispered in his ear, "How much is she per hour?" Charlie stood up and punched him in the face. The man told the police that he only asked Charlie if the empty chair next to him was available. But a witness came forward and said he overheard the man bragging that he was going to get Charlie to hit him and then sue him for a million dollars. No charges were filed against Charlie.

Despite the occasional drama, everyone in the front office in Oakland loved it when Charlie was in love. His calls were less stressful, and he was more courteous. One day Susan arrived at the Coliseum and showed off her one-carat engagement ring. We were all thrilled for her and Charlie. Alas, after a couple of months, Charlie stopped mentioning her name. We found out that he had found some love letters between her and a male Brazilian model. It broke Charlie's heart.

THE LAST STRAW

The Oakland A's compiled the worst record in the team's history in 1979. Like a duck, the franchise appeared to be floating along placidly, while under the surface its legs were pumping like crazy. The rebuilding continued, and the next season the team scored 109 more runs than in '79.

In March 1979, the City of Oakland and the County of Alameda filed a lawsuit in federal court claiming that Charlie had broken his lease by failing to "maintain an American League baseball team of the character and standing required by Major League rules for the conduct of professional Major League baseball games...." The suit was frivolous and amounted to harassment. Charlie denounced the suit as "bullshit" and moved the court to dismiss it. He explained what was obvious to anyone knowledgeable about baseball—that the rebuilding of the team was not aimed at 1979 but at 1980, an assertion that the results of the 1980 and '81 seasons bore out. The lawsuit was promptly dismissed, but for Charlie, exhausted from years of costly divorce, repeated heart attacks, and unremitting media abuse, it was the last straw.

CHAPTER 34

BILLY CLUB

1980

The phone rang at our Alameda home after midnight. Dad opened one eye and, seeing that it was still pitch black outside, decided he was dreaming and went back to sleep. A minute of silence passed. Ring! Ring! Ring!

Dad was now fully awake. A phone call at this ungodly hour could be from only one person. Dad, well-practiced in the art of grabbing the phone in the wee hours, swung his arm around and picked it up in one graceful motion.

"Hi, Charlie," he mumbled.

"Fix yourself a drink, Carl—we've done it again!" Charlie bellowed into the phone.

Carl could hear the ice cubes clinking against Charlie's glass of J&B.

"Charlie, it's not even eight in the morning in Chicago and you're already celebrating. So, I can assume dinner went well?"

"Carl, my boy, if it went any better, I'd check myself into a hospital!" Charlie yelled.

"So, when do I pick up Billy from the airport?"

"Great question!" Charlie yelled even louder. "Know what's a better one? What kind of beer should you bring him? You know he'll want a few for the ten-minute ride from baggage claim to the Coliseum!"

Charlie took a sip, barely noticing the silence.

"That was a joke, Carl. C'mon, this is our latest coup! This is exactly what will get the A's back on the front pages. Tell ya what, call me back when you find your sense of humor."

And with that, Charlie hung up.

Dad was too tired to be angry.

Groggy and yawning, I strolled into the bedroom, rubbing my bleary eyes. "Who was that?" I whispered.

"Well, honey, who else calls at this hour?"

My face brightened. "Charlie."

Dad gave his first smile of the day.

"I'll make some coffee," he said, patting me gently. "Today's gonna be a long one."

Carl was right. Charlie had done something nobody could have predicted just a half-dozen years earlier. He had hired a once bitter rival, Billy Martin. The same Billy Martin who ordered Lerrin LaGrow to throw intentionally at Campy Campaneris in Game Two of the 1972 ALCS. The same Billy Martin whom Charlie had publicly mocked with taunting messages on the Coliseum's scoreboard. The same Billy Martin who had been banished from the Yankees in the late 1950s after a drunken nightclub brawl involving his buddy Mickey Mantle. And the same Billy Martin who had quickly worn out his welcome in Minnesota, Detroit, Texas, and, most famously, back with the Yankees in the Bronx Zoo, where he, George Steinbrenner, and ex-Oaklander Reggie Jackson all famously clashed with each other. Billy Martin was available because Steinbrenner had fired him—again—in October of '79, after Martin had gotten into a fight with a marshmallow salesman in a Minnesota bar.

The rebuilding A's had young talent in the farm system and on the big-league club. Now, Charlie needed someone who was part manager and part miracle-worker to galvanize that young talent and build the new team. That someone, he hoped, was the erratic but inspiring Billy Martin. Billy came with a ton of baggage. He was known to bench, trade, demote, and release players because of personal grudges. His players called him a tyrant. But he was a great manager with a well-earned reputation for reviving struggling teams, taking them from worst to first almost overnight.

To fans and the press it looked like that meddling Charlie Finley was letting this great team fall apart. I resented the criticism, but I understood why it looked that way. Outsiders couldn't look "under the hood" to see what was really going on. Charlie and Dad could see the first signs of revival in 1979, but the fruits of their work wouldn't be apparent to the public until the 1980 season, so the criticism continued to pour down on the Finleys.

Dad found some welcome respect in one quarter, though. One day he was pulled over for by an Oakland traffic cop. The officer was getting ready to write up a citation, but when he realized who Dad was, he put his pad away, mounted his motorcycle, and escorted him to the stadium with lights flashing and siren blaring.

HURRICANE BILLY

Billy Martin had become the manager of the Minnesota Twins in 1969, eight years after his retirement as a player. The Twins had fallen on hard times just three years after nearly winning the 1965 World Series. But he was on borrowed time after a bar brawl in August, in which he beat up Dave Boswell, his star pitcher. Boswell was unable to play for two weeks, though he returned to win twenty games and lead the Twins to the playoffs. But the general manager, Calvin Griffith, and the rest of the front office were turned off by the Boswell brawl, and they fired Billy after his rookie season.

At every subsequent stop in his career—with the Detroit Tigers, the Texas Rangers, and the Yankees—Billy confirmed his reputation as a rascal, so it was only appropriate that he eventually landed with the

Oakland A's, whose roster of rascals was headed by Charlie O. Finley himself.

When Martin arrived at the Oakland airport, Dad found him wearing a black cowboy hat, sunglasses, and boots. He looked more like a NASCAR driver than baseball's bad boy—a down-to-earth kind of guy. After years of working for Charlie, Dad knew how to handle mercurial personalities. Billy, he figured, would be a breeze.

After a few minutes of small talk with Billy, Dad noticed a pretty teenage girl with black hair and olive skin who seemed to be with him—presumably Billy's daughter. When Billy realized he hadn't introduced her, he said, "Carl, let me introduce you to my wife, Heather." Shaking her hand, Dad thought, "*Wife?* He didn't say 'wife,' did he?" After a few niceties, Billy and his young bride left to get a bite to eat.

When Dad came home that evening, he announced it was a done deal—Billy Martin would be working for us. He told me that Billy's good friend, Mickey Morabito, would be coming with him—at Billy's request—as our new traveling secretary. Billy was known for his loyalty to friends.

Then Dad told me about Heather. She was sixteen; Billy was in his fifties. Wow. I was twenty-one. Billy was close to Dad's age. This was difficult to comprehend. Then it occurred to me I would have someone to pal around with and sit with during the games. Dad, however, had different ideas about that.

March 1980 was busy, as always, getting ready for opening day the first week of April.

I learned that some other A's employees had already met Heather. "Have you seen the rock on her finger?" they were all asking. I was told to be sure and look at Heather's left hand when we met. It was clear, though, that Dad really didn't want me to get acquainted with Heather. She was in the area for about two months before I finally met her.

I usually left games before the ninth inning to avoid the traffic, but I had heard that Heather waited for Billy in one the front offices, and one night I decided to stay until the game was over and meet her. I found the office and went in. There was Heather, alone. She seemed more mature than her sixteen or seventeen years, and despite her reputation as a take-charge person when it came to Billy, she had a shy quality about her. I completely forgot to look at her ring finger. Our visit was pleasant but brief, since the Coliseum was closing.

Later, I learned Heather had a reserved seat for each home game behind the dugout. Billy wanted to be able to see her, and if she wasn't in her seat when the game started, he freaked out and wouldn't calm down until she arrived. Nevertheless, it was well known that Billy was not averse to a little hanky-panky with women. At the same time he was living with Heather, he was seen coming out of his office with a big smile followed by a woman named Jill. She was dating one of the players in the lineup, who asked the pitcher Brian Kingman how you complain to the manager who is hitting on your girlfriend. In the end, Martin married Jill and dropped Heather. It broke Heather's heart, and we all felt sorry for her.

Brian Kingman might not have been the best source of advice about how to deal with Billy Martin, since his relationship with the temperamental manager was, shall we say, difficult. Billy insisted that players clear their plans to marry with him. When Kingman asked for permission to wed, Billy admonished him that his marriage had better not distract him from his pitching. Kingman married and lost the next nine games he pitched (en route to losing a record-setting twenty games that season).

Like many other players on the team, Kingman had a history of subtle, and not so subtle, conflict with Billy. In one game, Billy came to the mound and told him to walk the batter. Kingman threw three balls, but the batter reached out and smacked the fourth ball for a single. Billy came charging out of the dugout yelling "You mother-f—er! I told you to walk him!"—a correction that was clearly audible in the stands.

On another occasion Kingman threw a fastball that was promptly hit out of the park. Again, Billy stormed out to the mound, loudly berating Kingman for throwing a fastball. But it was Billy's own rule that, under the circumstances in which Kingman had found himself, the pitcher was supposed to throw all fastballs. Kingman and Martin exchanged insults, and the next day the sports headlines read, "Kingman

Rips Martin!" The pitcher says his relationship with Billy quickly "went south" and stayed there for his last two years with the team.

There's no question that in his own, eccentric way Martin helped energize some of the new young recruits on the roster. Some books give Martin all the credit for lifting the team. But the team had been rebuilding since 1977. The team had already begun rising in the standings before Martin signed on. One could say Martin was the final ingredient.

CHAPTER 35

BILLY BALL

1980

I n 1980 geologists detected signals that something big was about to happen. What they called "harmonic tremors" in the long-dormant volcano Mount St. Helens pointed to the catastrophic eruption that followed in May. That spring, seven hundred miles to the south, the Oakland A's were giving off harmonic tremors of their own.

The antithesis of Ernie Mehl was the *Oakland Tribune*'s Ralph Wiley, a talented sportswriter with integrity who shilled for nobody. He didn't have to. Respected as a consummate pro, he sprinkled his daily game coverage with creativity and wit. In March 1980, Wiley set up shop in Scottsdale, Arizona, with the A's. And amid the relative anonymity of the Cactus League's meaningless games under a punishing desert sun, Wiley recognized before anyone else that the A's were about to perform a baseball miracle.

Billy Martin had been appointed GM as well as team manager. In Mesa, there was a sense that Charlie and Dad were handing him a whole new roster loaded with talent. Could he pull it all together? Wiley thought he could. He saw Martin take twenty-one-year-old Rickey Henderson under his wing, teaching him about the nuances of base-stealing, setting him on the road to the Hall of Fame.

The A's opened the 1980 season at the Coliseum against the first big-league team Billy ever managed: the Minnesota Twins. At first glance, they seemed to be the same old hapless A's. The box score looked like the Twinkies roughed up Langford, Oakland's opening night starter, and squeaked out a 9–7 win in extra innings.

But anyone among the 24,415 A's die-hards could see this was a different team—flawed but hungry and full of fight. The Twins jumped out to a 5–0 lead that seemed insurmountable for a bad team, but the A's were no longer a joke. In the seventh inning they stormed back, scoring seven runs on the hot bats of their young, talented outfield: Rickey Henderson, Dwayne Murphy and Tony Armas. In the end, they couldn't overcome their biggest weakness, the bullpen. "Spacey" Bob Lacey, the A's closer, blew the lead in the ninth, and the game went into extra innings before the A's lost 9–7 in the twelfth. They lost a couple more, and after five games, they were an ordinary 2–3.

But then it started. Boosted by that stellar starting pitching, Billy's A's ripped off seven consecutive wins. Five weeks into the season, the Green and Gold was in first place, shocking the baseball world. But it wasn't just the W's they were hanging, it was *how* they were doing it. Martin was pulling out every trick he could think of, using Henderson's all-world speed to steal bases, calling suicide squeezes, double steals— anything he could think of to steal a win. Martin was putting on a clinic on how a manager gets his team to overachieve. The controversies in other cities, especially in New York, had obscured the fact that he was one of the game's best skippers. "They laughed when Charlie Finley hired Billy Martin," wrote Wiley in the *Tribune*. "He has brought them respectability without a quality second baseman or shortstop and without a bullpen."

Billy had infused the team with his scrappy, never-say-die spirit, but now the poor student from West Berkeley was getting credit for something new—outsmarting people. That's exactly what he and his A's were doing. They were outwitting opponents as much as defeating them on the field, and they started getting inside their heads. Wiley went on to quote a Cleveland Indians scout who said, "Martin maneuvers his players and is always looking ahead. Give him nine guys and he'll fight you to the finish even if the talent is mediocre." The undertalented scrapper, the bar brawler, had become baseball's master tactician.

Even when stars like Henderson and the starting pitchers faltered, Martin was squeezing every ounce of limited talent out of players like Mickey Klutts and Shooty Babbit. The motley, uneven roster inspired Wiley to write, "Martin's commando style has produced 13 double steals, one triple steal, seven steals of a home in 13 attempts and 13 suicide squeezes in 19 tries."

Wiley coined a phrase that would become part of baseball lore: "The A's are a kind of exhilaration not because of a man, but because of an attitude. Billy Ball. If it were a fever, the A's would be an epidemic. There's another name for it. Confidence."

The A's incredible turnaround made a great story, and Martin's boys electrified Bay Area sports fans. Even the East Coast media started to take notice, with New York's beat writers fascinated to see how their prodigal son was faring on the Left Coast.

As Billy Ball became a national sensation, Charles O. Finley's calculated risk to hire Martin was beginning to look like yet another brilliant move. "I thought to myself, 'By God, the old S.O.B. has done it again,'" said Ron Bergman, the former *Oakland Tribune* beat writer. Like most baseball insiders, Bergman knew that the mad genius had hired Billy to microwave the franchise—make it instantly hot so that buyers would not only want the team but be willing to raise their offer.

The summer of 1980 unfolded exactly the way that Charlie had envisioned. Bergman was right: the old S.O.B. really had pulled off one last trick.

Well, maybe not the last.

CHAPTER 36

CHARLIE FIRES AND CARL REHIRES

1979-1980

Nothing revealed how much Billy Martin's A's had captured the Bay Area's imagination more than the attendance figures. The A's were baseball's worst team in 1979, going 54–108. But they were even worse in the box office, selling an unthinkably paltry 306,763 tickets.

The next year—Billy's first as A's manager—Oakland went 83–79 and drew 842,259 fans, an increase of more than half a million. Midway through the 1980 campaign, the attendance boost was right in line with the improved record, and Charlie wanted to thank his new skipper for both successes. He held a "Billy Martin Day" at the Coliseum in August.

Charlie wanted it to be first-class all the way, so he invited Billy's old friends and teammates, Mickey Mantle, Whitey Ford, and Joe DiMaggio to his box seats. Each was a Yankee legend and, except for DiMaggio, an old drinking buddy of Billy's.

JOB SECURITY

When twenty-three-year-old Ted Robinson applied for a job on the A's staff, Charlie sent him to the Oakland front office and told him to report to Carl Finley, who ran the show out there. This wasn't going to be Robinson's dream job, but he came away with fond memories, especially of Dad. Robinson was going to be in charge of getting Billy Martin and his friends onto the field in time for the pre-game ceremony.

One afternoon at the Coliseum, Robinson recalls, Charlie hosted the American League president, Lee MacPhail, in the owner's box, in the loge section between the second and third decks. Charlie repeatedly called Robinson up to the box, making special requests for food and drinks that the franchise back then simply didn't have handy. When Robinson failed to produce the desired refreshments, the team owner exploded and fired Robinson on the spot, in front of MacPhail. A crestfallen Robinson trudged back to the front office. What was he going to tell his parents? Or his girlfriend? First things first, he went to say goodbye to Carl.

"What do you mean, you have to go?" Carl asked. "I've been fired," Robinson said. "Charlie fired me." "Well, you're re-hired," Carl said with a reassuring smile and a pat on the back. "Don't worry, Charlie will forget this ever happened. You still have a job, Ted." And with that, Robinson went back to work. Nearly thirty-five years later, Robinson remembers being "fired" by Charlie more than once that summer, and each time Dad hired him back. "I loved Carl," Robinson recalls. "He always had my back and the backs of so many people who worked there."

Today, Robinson is the radio play-by-play announcer for the San Francisco 49ers and a sportscaster for NBC. His career in sports started with the Finley boys in Oakland. To this day, Robinson wonders what would have happened to him if not for Carl Finley's gentle leadership as his first boss. "I might not be where I am today if Carl hadn't stuck up for me all those times when Charlie fired me," he says.

OPTIMISM

The 1980 season ended for Billy Martin as the first "Rocky" movie did—with a bittersweet defeat but also with the pride and satisfaction of an underdog who has won respect. True to form, Martin's players fought and scrapped to the bitter end, long after the Kansas City Royals had eliminated them.

But for the A's, second place never looked so brilliant. After three years of being a laughingstock, the Green and Gold had again become a contender, a team always respected and sometimes feared. Martin, the short-tempered miracle worker, had been just as advertised, squeezing every last ounce of talent out of this team. He had even kept his famous blow-ups where they belonged—on the diamond. His on-field beefs with umpires enthralled the East Bay's underdog-loving fans, who roared from the grandstands whenever Billy went nose-to-nose with an umpire. His tantrums often got him ejected, but not before tossing his hat, kicking dirt on the plate or the umpire's shoes, and carrying on in the grand tradition of the national pastime.

Off the field in Oakland, Billy (as usual) was no saint, but as summer turned to autumn and then to a typically gray, rainy Bay Area winter, Billy and Oakland fans could enjoy something they hadn't had for a while—optimism. For Charlie, though, the '80 season would have nothing to do with his future with the A's. He was preparing to say good-bye.

CHAPTER 37

THE LAST FINLEY IN BASEBALL

1980

At a mid-summer game, I was in our box seats with Charlie. In the next box over, separated from us by a thick glass partition, were some of the Haas family, who were preparing to make a bid for the franchise. Charlie leaned toward me and, with his trademark rascal smile, whispered, "It's them against us." He said it in a playful way, just to see my reaction. Just then Dad popped in, and that moment was over.

"THEY CAN'T TAKE THAT AWAY FROM ME"

The phone rang in Dad's apartment at 5 a.m. Already up and in his suit and tie, watching the steam rise from his coffee, he looked at the phone for a few rings and finally picked up. "Is this the current owner of the Oakland A's or the former one?" he said, forcing back a laugh.

"Arnold Johnson's been dead for twenty years, so...," Charlie replied.

"Well then, Mr. Johnson, you've got the wrong number."

They both laughed a little.

"As of this morning, I'm still Charles Owner Finley. But as of tonight, that might be a different story."

"You know, I'll believe that when I see it," Dad replied. "You still love it too much." Charlie had no witty retort for that. The silence made dad uncomfortable. "Don't you?"

Charlie let out a big sigh before answering. "Well, I've got eleven million reasons to stop loving it."

"Not a bad deal," Dad said, remembering the sale would be for eleven million dollars. "Not bad, considering you had four million reasons to start. Not bad at all." Dad squinted. There was little life on the other end of the phone. "Um, Charlie—"

"Hey," Charlie interrupted, "I'm still gonna call you at five a.m., you old sonuvabitch."

There it is, Dad thought. Then, "And for some goddamm reason, I'll still answer," he replied.

"And they say I'm the crazy one," Charlie said, laughing. The laughter gave way to another lull, an especially long one.

"It was one helluva ride, wasn't it, pardner?"

"Three consecutive World Series titles...."

"Couldn'ta done it without ya, Carl."

"Five consecutive division titles...."

"The only non-Yankees dynasty in just about...forever!"

Another long pause and another big sigh.

"And," Charlie started to sing in a bad Sinatra impression, "They can't take that awaaaaaay from me!"

"You be good, Carl," he added. "But try to be bad a little more often, will ya?"

And with that, before Dad could reply, Charlie hung up.

CHARLIE SELLS THE FRANCHISE

By 1980 Dad was actively seeking potential buyers of the franchise. Working his many contacts, he finally attracted interest from Walter

Haas Jr., the CEO of Levi Strauss & Co. and a scion of one of San Francisco's wealthiest families. The sale went through in August, just as Billy Martin was dragging the A's back to respectability.

For Charlie, it was farewell to a dream. Despite all of the things he accomplished in life—self-made millionaire insurance man and father of seven, among other things—he would be known forever as the owner of the World Series–winning Oakland A's. He loved attention, even more than money or winning championships. And as intelligent as he was, he had to have known that the thing that brought him the most notoriety, being an MLB team owner, was going away.

Charles O. Finley was gone. But the pieces of *his* successful team were still there. Young star players like Rickey Henderson, Dwayne Murphy, and Mike Norris were making A's fans roar again at the Coliseum. And Charlie's manager, Billy Martin—that combustible baseball genius—was leading the improbable Green and Gold show to victories.

There was just one more notable holdover: Carl Finley, who had been there the longest. Haas and his family were successful business leaders, but they had never run a baseball franchise. They were smart enough to realize they might need to lean on someone like Dad, who had run the day-to-day franchise operations for nearly two decades. Dad was happy to oblige. In August 1980, it was a new A's era, with new owners, in a new decade. Dad wondered how strange it might feel being the only remaining Finley in baseball.

Andy Dolich remembers Carl Finley as "the master of having fourteen jobs" as he ran the A's front office, "each of which he did in spectacular fashion." Dolich became the A's director of marketing after Haas and his family took over. He was immediately impressed with Carl because "he never told you how busy he was like so many people do today," says Dolich, now a Bay Area sports business consultant.

Dolich was less impressed with the physical state of the A's front office in 1980, when he first saw it a few days after the sale was official. Dolich parked in the Oakland Coliseum parking lot, walked up the slight concrete hill, and entered the A's offices. The first thing he noticed was that nobody was there. Where a receptionist might sit, there was a steel cage desk—right out of an old film noir movie. A phone said "Dial 0 for assistance." Dolich dialed but there was no answer. He looked around the empty room and tested the knob of a sliding door. It was unlocked and opened into the switchboard room. "It was the kind of switchboard you'd see in Mayberry RFD," he said.

Dolich went to the next office, and nobody was there, either. This was getting eerie. Was he in the *right* Oakland Coliseum? He walked deeper into the suite and finally found signs of life. Wally Haas (the owner's son) and Roy Eisenhardt (Wally's brother-in-law) were sitting there. That was his first introduction to the A's front office.

Later in the day, he met Carl Finley and discovered how thinly staffed the front office was and how much weight fell on Carl's shoulders. "When I looked around, I was impressed with what was happening, not what wasn't happening," he recalls.

Carl wrote the daily game reports, communicated with Major League Baseball leaders, communicated with the A's baseball personnel, and dealt with employees on the business side, which included the "bat boy" M. C. Hammer.

"Who's taking care of the food? Who's leaving the comp tickets at Will Call? Where's the mechanical rabbit getting oiled up? Where's Charlie O the Mule sleeping? Carl took care of all of that," Dolich said.

After a few days in the Coliseum offices, Dolich noticed that there was a telephone in the front office's men's bathroom. This was at least twenty-five years before cell phones became omnipresent. He asked Carl, who shrugged with a smile, saying that if Charlie needed to talk or wanted updates on the ballgame that day, Carl could speak uninterruptedly.

"You could hear Charlie coming before you saw him," Dolich said. "That's when I realized the extent to which Carl could really compartmentalize his ego, his needs. Carl was never about himself. He understood that Charlie was always about Charlie. It takes a deft touch to navigate that, which Carl did."

"Carl had this beatific grin, like Pope Francis has, that seemed to say, 'I'm good, I know what's happening. I don't have to open my mouth to let you know what's happening.'"

BACK ON THE FARM

The 1981 A's became one of the great Cinderella stories in franchise history. But Charlie, the team's once and forever architect, was back on his Indiana farm and wouldn't even be there to see the renaissance of Oakland baseball.

CHAPTER 38

THE LAST FINLEY TEAM

1981

A lthough we no longer owned the franchise, we considered the 1981 Oakland A's our last team. That team had the greatest start to a season in the history of baseball and finished first in the American League West. It almost didn't matter that the season was interrupted by a players' strike.

It was the Haas family's first full season as the owners. More importantly, it was Billy Martin's second season as manager, and the fame of "Billy Ball" was about to peak. The A's were the talk of baseball.

Something was different off the field, too. Led by its marketing guru Andy Dolich, the front office was trying things that no other pro sports team had tried. Dolich promoted the "Billy Ball" brand that Martin embodied, mixing witty TV ads with relentless outreach to Bay Area households. As the team won and won, old A's fans—and plenty of new ones—came out in droves to the Coliseum.

As excited as everyone was to be back in the playoffs after a six-year drought, I can't say that I had fun. I was a kid during the World Series glory years, but in 1981 I was twenty-three. I had expectations and had developed a competitive streak. As the A's trailed 4–0 in Game Three of the American League Championship Series at the Oakland Coliseum, I was overcome with a frustration that I had never felt before when watching baseball. After two consecutive seasons in which the A's reached the playoffs, I sat there during the game second-guessing nearly all of Martin's moves, seething in anger that none of them, for once, was paying off. You could say that I was watching the game like any other die-hard A's fan, but that doesn't really capture it. I know what it's like to have the whole world hang on every swing of a bat, foul ball, base hit, line drive. It's the best and the most stressful feeling ever. Every base hit by the other team made me want to throw up. But every hit by our side didn't really make that feeling go away. In fact, I was watching the game as Charlie did, reacting to each pitch with all the childlike emotion that he used to.

When New York closer Goose Gossage got the last out and the Yankees celebrated on the Coliseum turf, I joined forty-seven thousand other A's fans in sorrow that night. None of us knew it at the time, but a major chapter in the franchise's history had just come to a close.

The fact is, the 1981 team was largely Charlie's roster—talent he and Dad had scouted and signed up in previous years. He had been, in fact, rebuilding the team, using his unique and successful intuitive methods. In 1980 Charlie and Dad had left Oakland and the new owners the foundation of a great team. What they did with it was, for the first time in twenty years, out of our hands.

The 1982 season was not as impressive, with a fifth-place finish, perhaps because Billy was seen selecting the lineup for some games by pulling names from a hat. Was that a sign of burnout?

FRONT OFFICE FINISH-OUT

All the years that we were in the Coliseum we had depressing, cold, unfinished cinderblock walls in our front offices. The Coliseum board never got around to fulfilling the promise it first made back in 1968 to finish out the offices. Charlie, as stubborn as his namesake mule, refused to put his own money into the stadium—he had learned his lesson in Kansas City—and the cinderblock walls remained unfinished. The new owners, however, had less tolerance for such Spartan surroundings. They reluctantly put up the money to finish the walls and floors and replace the overhead florescent lights. When they were done it was a lovely place.

CHAPTER 39

THE LAST PHONE CALL

1982

Many fans have asked me over the years whatever happened to Harvey the mechanical rabbit. Harvey had been installed in Kansas City in a shaft just behind the home plate umpire and would pop up with a big grin and a fresh baseball after a foul ball or homer. The grinning rabbit with the glowing red eyes followed the team to Oakland, where he continued to entertain fans, but after a few years he malfunctioned. Harvey could get only halfway up his home plate rabbit hole, and Dad never got around to having it repaired.

When Charlie sold the franchise, he asked Dad to do away with Harvey so he wouldn't be subject to ridicule by the media. Dad told me he rolled up his sleeves and smashed Harvey to little pieces with a baseball bat. I think it was some kind of grief ritual, Dad's saying good-bye to the times, but I felt so sad to hear what had happened to Harvey.

For years, Charlie called Dad every morning to talk about the state of the A's or what a sportswriter had said about Charlie or just to gossip. Once Charlie had sold the team, the phone calls were fewer and farther in between. Dad could tell that it bothered Charlie when the A's made the playoffs in '81 without him. He would remind Charlie that the team's success was tied to the talent they had drafted and signed in the mid-to-late 1970s, their coaches, their manager Billy Martin, and other key persons pulled up from their farm team or acquired in trades. Charlie may have been gone, but his and Dad's handiwork was still paying dividends for the Oakland A's.

MARTIN CRASHES

As the losses piled up in 1982, Billy Martin started to unravel. The manager had always been a wild card—a hard-drinking, insecure scrapper famous for coaxing unlikely wins from untalented rosters by day and a bar brawler by night. He was a local boy, having grown up on West Berkeley's mean streets in the 1940s. His hardscrabble origins led him to hate the wealthy kids from the Berkeley hills and those sophisticated college students at Cal. Unfortunately for Billy, the A's new owners—led by Walter Haas Jr., his son Wally Haas, and his son-in-law Roy Eisenhardt—were exactly like those UC Berkeley kids he grew up disliking.

"Why do they use all those big words?" Billy would complain to Dad over beers in his office. "Why do they want to talk all the time? Why don't they just leave me alone and let me do my job?" He had a hard time relating to people he thought talked down to him.

So while the season wound down, the lava in Billy's gut kept rising. At some point, something had to give. Among other things, Martin was heard yelling racial and other expletives from inside the offices.

One morning when Dad arrived at work, early as usual, he walked in to find the smashed remnants of Billy Martin's office—light fixtures torn from a wall, a wrecked desk and chairs, broken glass, and a TV with the screen kicked in. After pondering the scene for a moment, he picked up his hat and headed out. As he passed the receptionist's desk she mouthed the word "Billy."

Dad turned around and went back to his office, closed the door, and tried to dial Martin's office, on the hope that at least one phone was left working there. No luck. Then he dialed another number. "Charlie? That's right, you old sonuvabitch," Dad said with a big belly laugh. "Now, tell me exactly what you know about all this." He listened to Charlie's reply, then laughed again. The Finley rascals were talking once more about the inner workings of the Oakland A's. And for a moment, for both of them, all was right with the world again.

It was never clear why Martin destroyed his office. In any event, as with every other kind of mess in the front office, it was left to Dad to clean it all up. His classic understated smile briefly crossed his face, and he made some calls to get some help. A little later he returned with his camera and took half a dozen photos.

LONG AND MERITORIOUS SERVICE

Dad continued with the Athletics franchise for a few years after Charlie sold it. He was listed in the 1983 Club Directory as "Vice-President and General Counsel," the fourth of the sixty-seven names listed. He mentored the man who would eventually replace him, Richard Alderson, known as Sandy, the assistant to the president for baseball operations. Sandy shadowed Dad each day, observing and learning how things were run, and they frequently traveled together on franchise business. Dad remarked to me that he and Sandy had stimulating conversations and called him "really bright."

Although the A's would call on him for occasional help for several more years, Dad officially retired in 1984. At a dinner in New York, Major League Baseball presented him with a rare lifetime pass to all major league games. Lee MacPhail, president of the American League, and Chuck Feeney, president of the National League, signed it. The simple inscription on the gold-colored metal pass could not have been more fitting: "For Long and Meritorious Service."

CHAPTER 40

LEGACY

How did they do it?

An important part of Charlie's and Dad's legacy is the lessons they taught about building a winning team. Some of these lessons are obvious, but for a number of teams they're hidden in plain sight.

FARM TEAMS

Charlie and Dad understood from day one that the key to building a winning team was, quite simply, their *farm teams* in Birmingham, Vancouver, and Modesto. Yes, other owners gave their farm teams lip service. But Charlie and Dad understood, or quickly learned, that the farm team was not just one more thing to have to think about; it was the cornerstone of a successful franchise. Charlie said he planned ten years in advance. Today's teams, with all their frantic trading, seem to seek instant gratification. Not Charlie. Not Dad.

COACHES

Charlie and Dad discussed hiring our coaches in detail.

My husband has observed that some clubs trade players who haven't met the team's expectations, only to see those same players become stars on other teams. He speculates that it's because of the coaches. Some coaches cannot bring out the best in the players, and others can. I think a lot of the Finley success was due to our coaches. Our coaches sometimes worked in our front office during off-season.

TIME

Charlie would trade if a player's "chemistry" was not right, but he kept the core group of highly talented players together so long that anticipating what each other would do became a matter of instinct. The shortstop could throw to second base even if no one was there; he knew by habit exactly when the second baseman would get back to base. If players have good chemistry, leave it alone.

INSTINCT AND SCOUTING

Charlie had remarkable instinct. He could look a prospect in the eye and tell whether he was a winner or not, like a racehorse owner looking into a thoroughbred's eyes. He could see it in old players as well as young prospects. He could see potential in a player that others could not. You might say he had a "savant's" eye.

More than that, he could tell whether a player was a winner *in the moment*. His posture as he approached the batter's box. The look on his face while standing in the dugout observing the game. His gait as he ran out to center field. A quick call to the dugout from his office in Chicago.

Charlie did much of his own scouting and recruiting. Marvin Miller of the players' union marveled, "Finley is absolutely the best judge of baseball talent I've ever seen."

It has become conventional in Major League Baseball not to mention instinct. Winning or losing, it is thought, is largely a question of money, statistics, shrewd trading, and selling. For some it is only a business investment. We did not follow any of those paths. We took a different path to winning.

FANS

For us, the fans were always number one. We hosted special social events—which players were required to attend—for our season ticket holders. We sent out seventy-five thousand valentines to local high schools that served as free passes. We let fans go onto the field to pet Charlie O and have their photos taken with him. We gave discounts to seniors and students. We often sent Charlie O to visit children in the hospital. One of my occasional jobs was to circulate among the fans and tell them Charlie and Carl Finley say hello. As Rex Lardner wrote in *Life* in 1961, "It is doubtful if any owner or part owner has ever been as solicitous about the comfort of the fan or the peace of mind of his players, or has identified himself so closely with the success of his ball club."

"HELICOPTER" OWNER

According to Charlie's critics, he victimized his players, pressured them with unfair expectations, and argued with them about compensation. You'd think he locked them up in a prison called the World Series.

No. They stayed, they became winners, and they were proud of it.

Charlie and Dad gave them that gift.

Even today you'll hear it said that Charlie Finley was a "micro-manager." If more owners did a little more Finley-style micro-managing, Major League Baseball might have been spared some of the steroid scandals that have tarnished so many reputations. Charlie wanted to know every drug, including prescription drugs, that every player was taking. There were no suspensions on a Charlie Finley team.

I became convinced that Charlie's sitting behind our dugout contributed to the team's success. The players could not avoid or ignore Charlie as he scrutinized them with his famously intense dark eyes. They could feel his gaze on the backs of their necks. They knew that what they were doing on the field was important—Charlie was there.

Charlie was the original "helicopter" owner, hovering over the team while a game was on and keeping a phone line to the dugout close by. If this brings three consecutive World Series championships, what's wrong with it?

THE FINLEY ERA

From the day he beat out Ernie Mehl in buying the Kansas City Athletics, Charlie Finley had enemies in the press. And though he was the subject of journalistic animosity until he sold the team twenty years later, a lot of sportswriters recognized Charlie's visionary leadership and gave him credit.

In 1995, Dave Newhouse wrote in the *Oakland Tribune* that "Finley had an uncanny eye for talent." He also said that Charlie deserves a place on the Coliseum wall, like a jersey tribute.

Garrett Smalley Jr., the editor of the *Daily Record*, recognized how far Charlie brought the team: "It wasn't only in the checkbook that the A's were deficient. They were bankrupt in players, managing, farm team system and even front-office personnel. [Arnold] Johnson had gutted the team sending their best to the Yankees and pocketing the money.

"Finley was no fool. Indeed, it turned out he was a baseball genius. He turned that pitiful rag-tag bunch of baseball castoffs into a respectable organization."

The men who played and managed for Charlie agreed. Speaking at Charlie's funeral in 1996, Reggie Jackson looked back: "He was a tough guy and I learned a lot about demanding excellence and that helped mold my career…. [T]he difficulties improved us and we became better people." After the funeral, Reggie added, "[W]hen times caught up with his thoughts, he became an innovator and creative." Dick Williams, the former manager, also at the funeral, remarked, "He was a great man. The farther you go away from him, the more you realized it. The man was a genius."

That same year, the lawyer and sportswriter Jay Darby added a striking tribute: "Finley almost single-handedly saved baseball in the early 1970s with his showmanship and charisma, and ultimately, his love and understanding of the game. And, he built perhaps the best baseball team ever assembled, and changed the game for the better."

Reporting on a fortieth-anniversary reunion of the A's 1974 World Series–winning team, Daniel Brown of the *San Jose Mercury News* wondered why Oakland's "Moneyball" era gets all the attention:

> With apologies to Brad Pitt, members of the Swingin' A's wondered Friday night if Hollywood made a movie about the wrong team. For a real blockbuster about Oakland baseball, forget "Moneyball" and get a load of the Technicolor bunch that won three consecutive World Series from 1972–74.
>
> "It would have to be a seven-hour movie," reliever Rollie Fingers said.
>
> "It would have to be Rated-R for violence, language and all of the above," former pitcher John "Blue Moon" Odom said.
>
> "What would that title be? 'The Misfits'?" pitcher Vida Blue asked.[1]

CHARLIE THE MAN

It's not easy to sum up a life like Charlie's. He paid a huge price, his divorce, to accomplish what he did. So did my dad, my mom, and me. Money, careers, marriages, home...all were tossed into a blender and churned into a bitter, fabulous, steaming stew of crossed destinies.

Charlie was always honest and straight up front; there was no mystery where he stood on issues. He revealed his soft spot for people who just needed an opportunity when he brought fifty-nine-year old Satchel Paige back to pitch three innings, when he hired young Betty Caywood as the first woman announcer, and when he gave the microphone to Stanley Burrell (M. C. Hammer) and let him announce a few innings at the Coliseum. It was the same thing when he invited Marcy Bachman to be the first female reporter to cover the A's, when he signed Glenn Burke, the first openly-gay player in the big leagues, and when he opened his checkbook to make sure the kids on the staff of his groundskeeper George Toma were adequately paid and dressed.

Charlie was no one-dimensional baseball man. He, as they say, "had a life" outside of baseball. He was a thirty-second-degree Shriner and served as chairman of the National Tuberculosis Association's Christmas Seals campaign. In 1961 the White House honored him for his efforts on behalf of the National Tuberculosis Association. He donated substantial sums to local churches. In 1984 President Ronald Reagan honored him for his contributions to the Republican Presidential Task Force by dedicating an American flag in his name in a ceremony in the rotunda of the Capitol.

DAD

I know my father often wondered how life would have turned out if he had stayed in Dallas. He was just beginning the climb up the academic ladder when Charlie made that early Saturday morning phone call. He was thirty-seven and had never lived outside of Texas. He was the one who calmed things down, and the team and front office were often in need of calming down. He lived by the principle: Never let a small problem blossom into a huge problem.

LIFE LESSONS

What can we learn from Charlie Finley's baseball career? A number of things come to mind:

- Being the best invites envy, and a lot of people will want to see you fail.
- To be the best, you must be willing to pay the price—sometimes a very big price.

- Don't take the "high road" and ignore an unfair attack. Defend yourself!
- Don't dance on the dugout. You'll get hit with a foul ball.
- The path to being the best is often a very lonely road.
- Listen to your dad!

I remember a sign in Charlie's front yard at his home in La Porte: "Forget the Alarm. Beware of Owner."

▶ ▶ ▶ ◀ ◀ ◀

IT'S ABOUT THE BOY

The final question is: When Charlie looked in the mirror, what did he see? First, he saw a winner. If nothing else, he simply willed himself to be a winner.

He also saw a man who yearned for acceptance but didn't know how to achieve it. He saw a man who did not understand why he and his ideas were never admitted into the hallowed inner circle of Major League Baseball.

He saw a man who was, to the surprise of many, easily hurt by the unkind words of the sports media. He would try to brush it off with "At lease they spelled my name right." And over time, he began to say "That will give them something to hate." The more Charlie tried to impress baseball opinion-makers, the more vilification and criticism he got.

The A's Mike Epstein told an interviewer, "Charlie realized he might as well use the 'common enemy' to give the team a better unity. This way, the players would want to show him 'We'll win! You'll see!'"

But above all—as incongruous as it may seem—he saw a child. A child who felt that his mother didn't love him. Who loved running through the woods in Alabama. Who hated being poor. He saw a boy yearning to be a baseball player in the big leagues—hitting a long drive into the left field corner, careering around second, and sliding into third. Safe! He heard the stadium roar with approval.

He saw himself.

NOTES

CHAPTER 1

1. Merle Harmon, quoted in Matt Kelsey, "Remembering the World Champion 1962 Kansas City A's," Dec. 4, 2010, http://www.i70baseball.com/2010/12/04/remembering-the-world-champion-1962-kansas-city-a's/.

CHAPTER 6

1. David Brang and V. S. Ramachandran, "Survival of the Synesthesia Gene: Why Do People Hear Colors and Taste Words?," *PLoS Biol* 9(11): e1001205. doi:10.1371/journal.pbio.1001205. San Diego, La Jolla: Department of Psychology, University of California, November 22, 2011.

2. "The objectification of overlearned sequences: A new view of spatial sequence synesthesia"; David M. Eagleman, Department of Neuroscience, Baylor College of Medicine, Department of Psychiatry, Baylor College of Medicine: Houston, 2009. Journal homepage: www.elsevier.com/locate/cortex.

CHAPTER 13

1.   Hal Bodley, *USA Today*, August 13, 1993.

CHAPTER 23

1.   Bruce Markusen, "Card Corner: 1973 Topps: Mike Andrews," The Hardball Times, May 17, 2013, http://www.hardballtimes.com/card-corner-1973-topps-mike-andrews/.

2.   Donald Moore, "Oakland A's History: Finley Fires Andrews," Oakland Clubhouse, September 24, 2007, http://www.scout.com/mlb/athletics/story/683126-oakland-a-s-history-finley-fires-andrews.

3.   Billy Witz, "Second Basemen Joined by Time and Miscues," *New York Times*, October 17, 2010, http://www.nytimes.com/2010/10/17/sports/17andrews.html.

4.   Saul Wisnia, "Mike Andrews," Society for American Baseball Research, http://sabr.org/bioproj/person/7f1f5b41.

CHAPTER 29

1.   Hal Bodley, "Finley: Maverick Turned Prophet," *USA Today*, August 13, 1993.

CHAPTER 31

1.   Jerome Holtzman, "Finley-Kuhn: That Was Drama," *Chicago Tribune*, July 19, 1992, http://articles.chicagotribune.com/1992-07-19/sports/9203050272_1_charlie-finley-new-trial-commissioner-bowie-kuhn.

CHAPTER 32

1.   Bowie Kuhn, *Hardball: The Education of a Baseball Commissioner* (New York: Times Books, 1987).

CHAPTER 40

1.   Daniel Brown, "Oakland Athletics were perfect misfits in the early 1970s," *San Jose Mercury News*, May 30, 2014, http://www.mercurynews.com/athletics/ci_25870418/oakland-athletics-were-perfect-misfits-early-1970s.

INDEX